Upper To' Gallants and Rusty Scuppers

UPPER TO'GALLANTS
and
RUSTY SCUPPERS
adventures of an amateur mariner

H. Peale Haldt Jr.
with
Harry P. Haldt III

Haley's
Athol, Massachusetts

Copyright 2020 by Harry P. Haldt III.

All rights reserved. With the exception of short excerpts in a review or critical article, no part of this book may be re-produced by any means, including information storage and retrieval or photocopying equipment, without written permission of the publisher, Haley's.

Edited by Harry P. Haldt III.
Copy edited by Mary-Ann DeVita Palmieri.

Images in *Upper To'gallants and Rusty Scuppers* assembled by Harry P. Haldt III from photos, documents, and memorabilia in the collection of the late H. Peale Haldt Jr.

Haley's
488 South Main Street
Athol, MA 01331
haley.antique@verizon.net

Library of Congress Cataloging-in-Publication Data
Names: Haldt, H. Peale, Jr., 1916-2000, author. | Haldt, Harry P., III, 1946- editor.
Title: Upper to'gallants and rusty scuppers : adventures of an amateur mariner / H Peale Haldt Jr., with Harry P. Haldt III.
Other titles: Upper topgallants and rusty scuppers, adventures of an amateur mariner
Description: Athol, MA : Haley's, [2020] | Summary: "H Peale Haldt Jr relates his experiences as a deckhand during his prep school and college summers aboard vessels from a freighter to a four-masted schooner during the 1930s. Aboard the four-masted barque *Sea Cloud*, the largest private sailing yacht in the world, he meets Nedenia Hutton, later the actress Dina Merrill, daughter of Marjorie Merriweather Post Close Hutton Davies, owner of *Sea Cloud*. *Upper To'gallants and Rusty Scuppers* includes Dina Merrill's letters to Peale, who also sailed around the world aboard the President Lines *President Harrison* during the summer of 1939, as the world prepared for war"-- Provided by publisher.
Identifiers: LCCN 2019038713 (print) | LCCN 2019038714 (ebook) | ISBN 9781948380089 (trade paperback) | ISBN 9781948380126 (pdf)
Subjects: LCSH: Haldt, H. Peale, Jr., 1916-2000--Travels. | Seafaring life--History--20th century. | Sailors--United States--Biography. | Merchant marine--United States--Biography. | *Ringfond* (Ship) | *George B. Cluett* (Schooner) | *President Harrison* (Steamship) | *Sea Cloud* (Yacht) | Merrill, Dina--Correspondence. | Voyages and travels.
Classification: LCC G530.H175 A3 2020 (print) | LCC G530.H175 (ebook) | DDC 910.4092 [B]--dc23
LC record available at https://lccn.loc.gov/2019038713
LC ebook record available at https://lccn.loc.gov/2019038714

in memory of my father
and of stories of his days as a youth
working on ships at sea in the 1930s
—Captain Harry P. Haldt III
US Navy (Retired)

*To find adventures, you have to go out and look for them.
They don't ordinarily come to him who waits.*
—unknown

*Twenty years from now you will be more disappointed by
the things that you didn't do than by the ones you did do.
So throw off the bowlines. Sail away from the safe harbor.
Catch the trade winds in your sails.
Explore. Dream. Discover.*
—Mark Twain

Contents

Finding Upper To'gallants and
    Rusty Scuppers, a preface xi
Sailing the High Seas after
    Growing Up in a Salty Atmosphere, an introduction 1
Upper To'gallants and Rusty Scuppers: . . . .
    adventures of an amateur mariner 5
D/S *Ringfond* 7
George B. Cluett. 25
Sea Cloud 53
SS *President Harrison*. 91
Join Me While I Peel Off
    Forty-Six Years, an epilogue 149
Comparison of Ship Characteristics 153
Transcriptions from Entries in Peale's Logbooks 155
Experiencing What My Father Did, a postscript 163
An Unlikely Correspondence: letters to Peale from
    Nedenia Hutton, later the movie star Dina Merrill 165
Definitions. 189
Acknowledgments 193
About the Author and Editor 195
Colophon. 197

Finding *Upper To' Gallants and Rusty Scuppers*
a preface by Captain Harry P. Haldt III, United States Navy (retired)

*Captain Harry P. Haldt III
US Navy (retired)*

workaway . . . Indian Tickle
Charlie North . . . port fore
upper tops'l . . . owner's daughter
horseshoe barber . . . pit boss
Tower of Silence

Where do I begin?

As we got ready for a big yard sale, my wife and I went through an accumulation of items in our basement that we neither had use for nor room to store any longer. Among them we found boxes my mother had given me when she cleaned house years ago. As I recall, I then looked at them briefly, told myself I would go through them in detail later, and promptly forgot them.

But in the workup for the yard sale, Susan said we should look through a few of those family boxes. They included a small metal trunk with records and photos of ancestors, a box of old photo albums, letters and memorabilia from my father's World War II service, a box of dog-eared folders, old register books, my parents' wedding album, and a box of mementoes from my school life that my mother had accumulated meticulously, starting with a nursery school report card through to my college graduation program.

Susan and I started with the innocent looking box of folders, old register books, and the wedding album. Susan began with the album. I started looking through the folders—Nye Family, Colgate University fiftieth reunion, *Sea Cloud* cruise, MacArthur . . .

Why do I tell you all this? Because inside that box I found a folder labeled "STORY." Actually, the full label is "STORY written by HPH Jr." I pulled it out, opened it up, and started reading. I got a few pages in, put the folder down, and looked through the rest of the box. The old register books turned out to be records of trips my father took from 1931 to 1939. He had kept hand-written, detailed log books of sea voyages and ships he worked on during summers in high school and college years. As I read further, I matched chapters in the story with corresponding log books. A fascinating picture emerged.

I had heard stories from my father about his time at sea but only little snippets here and there. Four generations of our family have been connected to the sea from my schooner-fleet-owning great grandfather, Louis Harlow Haldt of Philadelphia, to me, a captain in the US Navy. According to a list in the folder, my father went to sea, on what the family called summer trips, seven out of nine years during the 1930s. Since he was born in September 1916, that meant he went to sea on his first trip at fourteen. Imagine yourself or one of your children working for the summer on a small tramp steamer heading for the West Indies at fourteen! I couldn't.

Stuck in the back of one of the log books I found a letter written by my grandfather to his son, my father, as Dad got ready to sail to Europe for a summer trip in 1932. Mind you, my father was only fifteen that summer, going overseas to bicycle around Holland by himself. In that letter I found out *who* was behind it, *what* was the plan, *where* did it lead, *why* my father started going to sea at fourteen, and *when* did it happen. The letter appears on page xv, and I will just let you read it without further explanation.

I finally understood. I saw my father in a totally different light. In the prologue of his story, Dad writes:

> Once in a while someone makes the mistake of asking me about those days. I fill up my glass, stare off into the past, and tell another

tale. One of the reasons that I still have a few friends left is because I know when to stop talking. One, or at the most, three stories are usually enough as long as they are appropriate to the conversation going on at the time. That trite old expression has come up so many, many times: "These stories are too good to die. Why don't you write a book?"

This is that book. My father wrote his story from 1984 to 1985 but why it stayed in the file, I do not know. Dad died in 2000. At one hundred, my mother does not remember Dad writing a story but does remember the trips he took all those years ago.

Did my father want me to find the file and lead me to start with the box containing the Story folder? I believe he did. I owe it to him to share his stories and not let them die. I have preserved my dad's words just as he wrote them, colorful as they are, even when perhaps a given reader would see them as inappropriate. Along the way I have added comments signed HPH III when I feel a bit more explanation might be useful.

I hope you enjoy *Upper To'gallants and Rusty Scuppers* about my father's fondest memories from his first job on the held-together-by-rust freighter *Ringfond* to his time aboard the beautiful square rigger *Sea Cloud*. I certainly have enjoyed reading them and bringing them to you.

Dear Peale —

I will not attempt much of a lecture and will try to keep the little word "DON'T" in the background so here goes.

Once upon a time there was a 'ittle bitsa baby boy whose mama and papa figured he had a little more horse sense than most youngsters his age (even if he did have some troubles in getting started in Latin!)

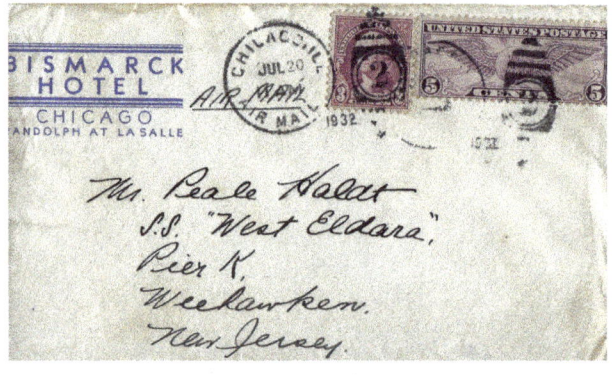

first page of letter, with envelope, from Harry P. Haldt Sr. to Peale on the occasion of one of the younger man's summer sea voyages

Please Be Sure to Keep Your Log Every Day

letter from Harry P. Haldt Sr. to H. Peale Haldt Jr. on
the occasion of one 1930s summer sea voyage of H. Peale Haldt Jr.

*Harry P. Haldt Sr.,
sales manager
Franklin Baker
Coconut Division
General Foods*

*H. Peale Haldt Jr.,
called Peale,
sophomore
Boonton, New Jersey
High School*

Mr. Peale Haldt
SS *West Eldara*
Pier K
Weehawken, New Jersey

Dear Peale,

I will not attempt much of a lecture and will try to keep the little word *don't* in the background, so here goes.

Once upon a time there was a 'ittle bit o' baby boy whose mama and papa figured he had a little more horse sense than most youngsters his age (even if he did have some trouble getting started in Latin!). Anyway, they said the best way to get the most out of this world is to at least know what all is in it. So before he was fifteen, they sent him off on a trip to the West Indies. He came back apparently none the worse for wear. In fact he even seemed somewhat improved! So they nodded their heads and smiled wisely, giving each other a pat on the back and even going so far as to extend a pat on the 'ittle bit o' baby boy's head.

Then the following summer rolled around. In the meantime, the 'ittle bit o' baby boy grew and showed what they took to be still more good common sense. He did not do quite so many foolish things—his papa did not lose his temper so often over his actions as had been the case before. His mama did not have to take his part quite so much (there being not so much cause), and even his little sister seemed to enjoy him more. He took what looked like a little more interest in homework —get me right—not work around the place but home study! Found himself a very nice and sensible girl, learned to dance and keep himself fairly well cleaned up, and, to cap the climax, took quite an interest in track athletics and even became county champion hurdler.

Well, as I say, the next summer rolled around and these trusting parents packed their 'ittle bit o' baby boy up once more and started him off before he was sixteen on a trip to Europe, which, strange to say, neither of them had ever seen themselves!! On that trip, like the one previously, he saw all kinds of sights and learned how foolish people can be and into how much trouble their own actions can get them. But remember this 'ittle bit o' baby boy now not only had a little more than his share of horse sense but by this time also had a very sweet young lady whom he wanted to make believe he was a pretty decent sort of a fellow. So once more he came back from his trip without getting mixed up in any foolish difficulties.

Finally, on account of his manly—that is—gentlemanly actions, his papa and mama said to each other, "What a fine man we have made of this 'ittle bit o' baby boy. We are not only proud of him, but so is his girl, and he can also be proud of himself. We have sent him to the West Indies (1931), Holland (1932), South Africa (1933), England (1934), the Mediterranean (1935), Brazil (1936), on a Gloucester fisherman (1937), and Australia and 'round the world (1938), have put him through Dartmouth (without a condition in Latin), and even given him a year at a European university. So let us sit back now and watch him go ahead, and we will take a few trips ourselves. And that's that, for they all lived happily ever after!

Seems like I have written so much about some 'ittle bit o' baby boy, I have no more paper left to write you a farewell lecture. However, yesterday's letter to your ma outlined just about how I feel about your trip—what to do and somewhere near how to do it, so why bother you with more details?

Please be sure to keep up your log every day. You sure will get a kick out of it when you are older. Also see The Hague, Amsterdam, Edam, Vollendam, and the (wrong again) Zuider Zee. Write postals at least to Uncle Lou, Aunt Billie, Uncle Ern (E. W. Haldt/6142 Morton Street, Germantown, Philadelphia, Pennsylvania) and Uncle Bert. Also your principal.

So long and the best of luck.

Love, *Dad*

Send June a postal
c/o Camp WAWENOCK-OWAISSA
South Casco, Maine USA

PS
Just one "don't"—
Show the officers you are interested in their work but *don't* bother them.

Summer Sailing Trips of H. Peale Haldt Jr.

1931 • D/S *Ringfond*, small steamer
West Indies

1932 • SS *West Eldara*, liner
Holland

1933 • couldn't go to sea

1934 • *George B. Cluett*, schooner
Labrador and Newfoundland

1935 • couldn't go to sea

1936 • *Cornell*, fishing trawler
Georges Bank out of Boston

1937 • *Sea Cloud*, square rigger
Atlantic Ocean and Baltic Sea

1938 • SS *Black Hawk*, liner
bicycle tour of southern Britain

1939 • SS *President Harrison*, liner/freighter
around the world

Abbreviations D/S and SS in ship names stand for "steam ship"

Sailing the High Seas after Growing Up in a Salty Atmosphere

an introduction by H. Peale Haldt Jr., able-bodied seaman (retired)

H. Peale Haldt Jr., called Peale

The days when a farm kid could jam a hay fork into the nearest mow, pack up some underwear and a change of socks, and head for the nearest seaport are getting to be but memories that lead to daydreams. I, and I will apologize right now for the overuse of that personal pronoun, am one of the breed that is neither day nor night but belongs in that nebulous twilight that is halfway between.

As a high schooler in Boonton, New Jersey, an iron town in the hills of northern Jersey, I came from a line of salt water men. My grandfather was senior partner of Haldt & Cummins, a Philadelphia-based shipping company. As I write, a model of the three-masted trading schooner *Laura Haldt,* flagship of the fleet, sits on a table in my living room. (The model now sits on a bookcase in my living room. HPH III) Louis Harlow Haldt, my grandfather, made his fortune around the turn of the century owning schooners that plied the east coast from Nova Scotia to Mexico. What happened to him in 1929 is a sad and separate tale.

My dad, Harry Peale Haldt Sr., grew up in that world of commercial canvas sailing. As the owner's son, he shipped out to such faraway places as the Bay of Fundy, Newfoundland, Maine, and other areas on the coasters' routes. Dad ended up in the navy, naturally, during World War I. I was born about that time. He was stationed in Lewes, Delaware, protecting the coast from the U-boats, and Mother lived in Ridley Park, a suburb of Philadelphia, only a few hours away.

Louis Harlow Haldt, owner, Haldt Company, Philadelphia managing partner of Haldt & Cummins, Philadelphia

I grew up in an atmosphere of deepwater sailors. Our house had a stuffed blowfish, a huge dried starfish, dried seahorses, conch shells as door stops—I still have one at my basement door—ship models, and a million stories. As I grew up, I listened to tales my grandfather spun, stories Dad told about how he "won the war," what it was like in the fo'c'sle of a trader, and what the world is all about.

Ridley Park was and may still be a quiet bedroom community. It takes its place on the edge of the swamps between Chester and Philadelphia. The Great Baldwin Locomotive Works near Chester turned out steam engines almost like Detroit turned out cars.

model of the Laura Haldt, scale 176 to 1, flagship of the Haldt & Cummins fleet three-masted schooner Laura Haldt named after Louis Harlow Haldt's wife, Laura Built 1882 • 152.5 feet long at the water line • 35-foot beam • 13.5-foot draft Haldt & Cummins, owners with a ship's sextant, left

It was always the GreatBaldwinLocomotiveWorks in those days: you said it in one breath like "damnyankee" or "theothercity." There was the historic Eddystone Light. The locomotive works, the

HALDT & CUMMINS,
COMMISSION MERCHANTS
AND
SHIP BROKERS.

226 WALNUT STREET,

CABLE
"HALDT"
PHILADELPHIA.

business card for Haldt & Cummins

Eddystone light, and the swamp are all gone now. So, too, are the days when one of the captains would bring a barrel of fresh oysters to my granddad. A wooden barrel, top hoop loosened to hold down a wet burlap bag full of oysters, would be iced and stored in the dirt-floor cellar.

They were cellars in those days, not basements or rec rooms. The ice wagon came by three times a week, and we always had a yellow card in the kitchen window which meant "Stop—we need ice." My job, as I recall, was to direct the iceman to the cellar so we could ice down oysters when we had them. Then would come evening when my mother, my granddad, and I would eat the chilled half shells as fast as my granddad, Baba, could open them. My dad somehow never appreciated the succulent flavor of fresh, iced Chincoteagues, which was just as well, since it meant more for the rest of us.

So I grew up in that salty atmosphere. It was correctly assumed that I was born with salt in my veins. That natural phenomenon showed itself while I was in grade school. My favorite book was *Moby Dick or The White Whale* and my second favorite was Dana's *Two Years Before the Mast*. The latter was my bible. Later on, when I shipped out along the Labrador coast and still later when I was foremast captain on the four-masted barque *Sea Cloud*, I must truly say that those two books made a better canvasback out of me than if I had to have it beaten into me by some bucko mate.

During the years that followed, my salty blood came to the fore and, sure enough, I ended up shipping out during my summer vacations from high school and college. The adventures that follow are but memories now. Once in a while, someone makes the mistake of asking me about those days. I fill up my glass, stare off into the past, and tell another tale. One of the reasons I still have a few friends left is that I know when to stop talking. One, or at the most, three stories are usually enough as long as they are appropriate to the conversation going on at the time.

That trite old expression has come up so many, many times—"These stories are too good to die. Why don't you write a book?"

Well, friend, you can see why I shouldn't write a book. The depth of Shakespeare, the humor of O. Henry, the skill of Hemingway, the imagination of Asimov, the vocabulary of Howard Cosell—all have managed to escape me. But it is the telling of the following tales I really do enjoy.

So, perhaps, you would like to join me. You know that you can close the book, put it down, and come back to it any time you want me to ramble on about sailing among icebergs off Labrador or eating broiled grasshoppers in the Philippines or the Swede from the D/S *Ringfond* who wore six pairs of silk panties under his trousers when he had shore leave.

I hope you enjoy the following stories as much as I enjoy telling them to you.

Upper To'gallants and Rusty Scuppers

adventures of an amateur mariner

D/S *Ringfond*
built in Leirvik, Norway in 1901
length 171 feet • beam 28 feet • draft 15 feet
speed 7. 5 knots
June 4-July 27, 1931

cover of the log book Peale kept during
his summer working cruise aboard D/S Ringfond with sample log entries following
• transcriptions begin on page 155 •

FIRST ENTRY

Thursday 4 1931
Left Hoboken on ship "Kingford". Picked up freight at dock at Franklin Baker Coconut Co. Shoved off at about 4:30. Passed Coney Island at 9:05. We have full privileges on the ship, fore - aft and all over. Captain showed us around the ship. Dropped pilot at about 9:56. The boat is taking the swells swell. Good nite till tomorrow.

Friday 5, 1931
We didn't sleep very well last nite. The watch came and there out we went at about 1:00 A.M. The Captain B. mick, pronounced Bimick, came out. He is a swell guy, no kidder. About 7:30 we sighted an old 4 master with a steam of the United Fruit Co. We just came back from a stroll around the ship. Heard sighted serve and have a bunch of porpoises. Ran for our cameras. Saw was off the land but still we tried. The school passed

Saturday. Woke up dreaming that I was drowning but found out that rain was coming in the port hole and I was soaked. I was so tired that I didn't feel like getting up but a big clap of thunder changed my mind for me. It was raining "cats & dogs" but I couldn't find any. I put on my slicker and was standing by the rail holding it when W H A M
 O O O boy!! The lightning struck the water and the ship at the same time. My fourth felt like I swallowed a quart of battery juice, my hands were tingeling and I was scared. After that the rain eased up a bit and so I went up on the bridg. ... gave me a big bunch of bananas ... then they all turned

Wednesday. Woke up 8:00 Went down to the steward till 8:00 Had breakfast at 8:30. Came upon the bridge till 10:00 Went aft and talked with the chief. Stayed there till noon. During that morning 6 ships have passed us. Had dinner at 12:30. Came up on bridge till 4:00. Was watching the other ships thru the glass. Passed 3 more ships. Went down in the engine room. till 5:00. Went down in salon till 6:30. Ate dinner 6:45. Went down in to the boiler room till 8:30. Boy that's a very nice little place to play in. There you st[and] with nothing on except pants, shoes and a pair of gloves. The t[wo] hot furnaces are blazing with the refreshing heat of 200 F or [more] in front of you. The bunker is soft, fine and "mucha dirty" a[nd] on both sides and you stand there shoveling that same mat[erial] into the mouths of these ever-hungry furnaces at the rate of 25,600 ounces per two hours with an ordin[ary] iron shovel that has a wooden handle. When you st[and] [shoveling] you have to sit on a stack of blotters beca[use]

D/S Ringfond, a small coastal freighter at dock

D/S *Ringfond*

My first trip put me aboard the D/S *Ringfond* out of Norway. I was signed on as a workaway. A workaway is a green hand there to learn the business. In return for the opportunity to learn, he doesn't get paid.

The tramp steamer D/S *Ringfond* was of pre World War I vintage and was afloat, I sincerely believe, only because the layers of black and red paint made a thin skin of unsuspected value. One day outside Havana, several of us were chipping paint, an unending occupation that mates and bo'suns keep in reserve for the sunniest, hottest and least breezy days they can find. A chipping hammer is about the size and weight of a regular carpenter's hammer except that instead of a claw, it has a wedge-shaped chisel head used to chip off flakes of old paint. On the *Ringfond*, doing so afforded a supreme test of skill. One blow too hard or too direct lifted not only paint but also a rather large flake of the rusted deck.

Drinking

I was in high school at the time. Fourteen years old, as I look back. Pretty young. My sincere thanks to my mother and dad for letting me see the world from the deck of a deepwater ship. She sailed out of Hoboken, New Jersey, where I immediately learned there is a saloon or bar on every corner. Our course was to Havana,

Haiti, the Dominican Republic, Jamaica, and Corn Island off the coast of Nicaragua. We were taking general dry cargo down and were to bring back coconuts for the Franklin Baker plant. (My grandfather was a manager for Franklin Baker Coconut, a division of General Foods, and had direct access to the shipping business. HPH III)

My bunk in the fo'c'sle was typical, a narrow wooden bed with a side piece to keep you in place when heavy seas are running. The pillow had a unique smell all its own. Never before nor since have I found an odor quite like it: sort of a cross between wet chickens, eau du locker room, and diesel fuel. I got to like it so much, I actually missed it when I signed off.

Pre Castro Havana was a sailor's delight, and Harry's Bar was the place. Since they called me "the kid, Pete," my shipmates had to buy me my Cuba Libre, of course. My first man's drink. For reasons better understood now than then, my initial shore leave was short, direct, and very inexpensive.

Lesson #1 for this brand new merchant seaman:
Do not, repeat, do not try to match a Scowegian sailor drink for drink—
or for that matter, don't try to match any sailor!

Joy Girls

Port-au-Prince was my next foreign port. Now an experienced, tanned, muscular deck hand, I was ready to take on the world. As we warped in to the dock, we were just about head high to people on the pier, and here were several very handsome native girls waving a welcome to us.

"How very nice," I thought."Good public relations: a welcoming committee." As we drifted in and shoreside dock wallopers handled our lines, those lovely girls spoke to us. They had all sorts of plans as to how they would gladly spend the evening helping us get the most out of our hard-earned cash. They walked alongside our incoming freighter making deals left and right. I, with all of my worldly knowledge, was somewhat taken aback when one particularly attractive member of the welcoming committee looked me straight in the eye, winked, and smilingly said, " . . . an' don' worry about being too small . . . for the young ones, I get on top!" At my workaway wages, I was in no position to put her offer to the test.

Lesson #2: Joy Girls are the same the world over.
Leave your wallet on board, remove any identification, and
take along just what you plan to spend.

Barter

For a fourteen-year-old, I was learning fast.

One evening, Sven, who spoke only a few words of English, and I, whose total Swedish consisted of "tak-sa-maket" (my version of thank you), were going to go ashore. As we cleaned up and dressed in our shore clothes, I was shocked to see him put on ladies' silk panties one after the other until he wore about six pairs. When he pulled on his trousers, no one was any the wiser—except me. I have heard about pansies, fruits, or call them what you will, but not my shipmate, my friend!

Lord, if he should try to kiss me, I'd have to belt him one.

As we went down the gangplank, I allowed a safe distance between him and me while I tried to figure out just what it was he was up to. I had noticed that, even though he had splashed on some kind of sweet smellum, he at least had not put on any lipstick or rouge. I was learning fast. This country boy from the foothills of North Jersey was seeing the world through an altogether different set of glasses. (In the mid 1920s, Dad's family moved from Ridley Park, Pennsylvania, to Boonton, an old mill town in northern New Jersey, as my grandfather had a new position with General Foods in New York City. HPH III)

Later on, we were in one of Sven's favorite bars. I sat there, sipped my beer, and watched my friend greet all of his friends. Odd. Most of them were females. One in particular he introduced as his cousin. She was quite a bit more tanned than Sven, but it could be.

In no time, he went off with his cousin, having told the other girls to take care of me. They did, and I learned a lot about their homeland and their customs and began to get a buzz on from the beer. Pretty soon, Sven was back, happy as a man who had just finished a bottle of free rum—which he had, and somehow it was for free. Then he was off with one of his cousin's companions.

My friend was popular all right. He spent half the time with one of the girls or sitting at the scarred table buying me beers. I was still waiting and wondering what I'd do if and when he would suggest that he and I should go to one of those back rooms. Happily, he never did. We finished our drinks and went back to the ship. As Sven and I were undressing ready to sack in, I suddenly noticed that he no longer had on any of the silk panties.

Lesson #3: Never pay cash—barter!

Drunken Sailor

Had another lesson the next evening. One of the older men drank more rum than his brain could handle. When he returned to the ship, he was bleeding, staggering, and wearing no shoes. The gangway had one rope on the left side of the slatted walkway. He held it in his right hand and walked right off the pier.

One of my shipmates tied a line around my waist and lowered me over the side. I tied another line under his arms. He and I were hauled aboard, drained out, and sent forward to our bunks. Turned out he'd been Mickied. One loaded drink, and he was half out. To top it off, he was rolled of all his pay, which he had worked weeks to accumulate, and had his shoes stolen.

Lesson #4: Never go ashore by yourself. Go with a buddy.
The life of a Jack Tar was not all romance and wind-in-the-face.

Angry Shark

When people tell me fishing stories, I go along with them since I rather like fishing myself. But let someone start to monopolize the conversation and exaggerate his four-pound bass into a thirteen-pound monster, it's then I tell them this one.

Sharks like to follow ships. Garbage comes free and easy: no work for the little devils. One balmy afternoon, the first mate suggested we do some shark fishing. The chief engineer took a worn steel file about eighteen inches long, got it glowing hot in the main firebox, and hammered the file's tang into a circle around a six-foot length of chain. The other end he formed into a large hook. When it cooled, he cut a huge barb and finished it off by filing the ends into sharp points. The donkey engine got fed steam,

drawing by Peale during cruise on D/S Ringfond

the main boom swung around, and the chain with its huge hook got fastened to the end of the cable normally used with the boom to load or unload the cargo. Finally, Cookie gave us a piece of salt pork about the size of a softball. This we tied up in a red bandanna and jammed over the barb on the hook.

Experienced shark fishermen will confirm that sharks are able to "smell" the salt pork. The red bandanna serves to attract the shark's eye. With a twist of the controls, the boom swung outboard, the wire cable was let out, and soon we were hanging over the stern rail waiting to see what would happen.

It happened soon enough. We didn't see a thing, but the whole ship shuddered a little, actually listed a bit, and the wire tightened up so it hummed through the water.

Much shouting. The winchman reeled in the wire, and pretty soon there hung a writhing, jerking, very angry shark. The winchman swung him inboard and lowered him to the deck. The hook was well set, and Mr. Shark was doing his best to shake it loose or better still to tear our ship apart. Some of the braver hands were beating him with two-by-fours.

"Hit him on the nose. He's weakest there!"

"Hit him between the eyes. His brain is there!"

When the gnashing teeth cut one two-by-four into three pieces, one to the left of its head, one to the right, and a third in its mouth, that was too much for the interested but wisely non-participating captain. He went below and soon reappeared with an ancient but still serviceable rifle. He told us to get out of the way and then started blasting.

I had a faint feeling. Having on several occasions done considerable damage to the deck plates with my chipping hammer, I couldn't help but secretly wonder how much of the high-powered ricochets the poor *Ringfond* could take.

Sharks die slowly. It wasn't until the next day that any of us had the courage to tentatively kick it to see if it still moved. It didn't, so we had shark steak and liver for several days. Sharks' teeth were popular souvenirs.

But the smell! That shark had the last laugh, if sharks have souls. It could have looked out of its heavenly aquarium and enjoyed watching us hose down the deck several times a day for the next week or so trying to get rid of the worst stench—stench? hell no, *stink*—that I have ever smelled.

Lesson #5: *Never try to out-tale a tale-telling sailor.*

The difference between this and the thirteen-pound bass is that every word about our shark hunt is true.

Man o' War

Dugout canoes were not as scarce as one might imagine. In Jamaica while shelling on the beach, I came across a beached dugout that an older fisherman used every day to scratch out a living. He saw me admiring his canoe, so he wandered over and asked if I would like to go for a ride. It was an outrigger, so I was confident I could sit in it and paddle without capsizing.

Turned out I could and did paddle without tipping over, that is. The canoe was a beautiful work of art. Must have been nearly as old as the fisherman whose lined face and toothless mouth put him well above the thirty mark. The boat had some water in it, not from leaks but just general water that slopped over the low freeboard. I sat on the bottom, and the old man sat in the stern. We paddled around a bit, and as we did so, I began to get a terrible itch in my nether regions. I couldn't imagine what it was. All I knew was that with each passing moment the itch turned from just that into a very severe pain.

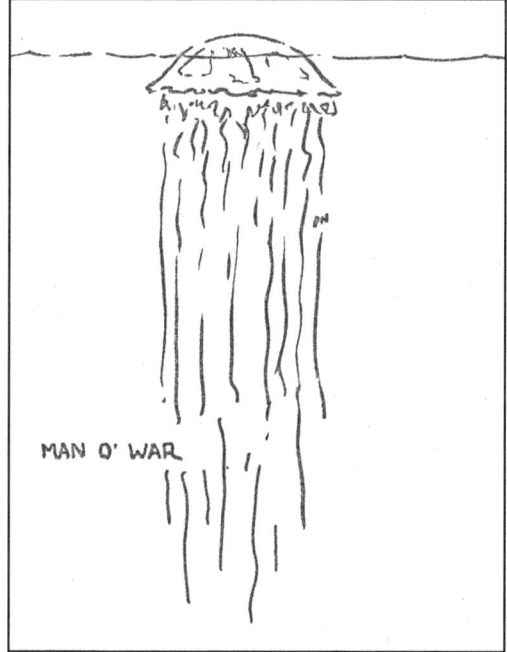

drawing by Peale during cruise on D/S Ringfond

Finally, I told the fisherman about it. He sort of snapped his finger and said, "I forgot. Just before I came in I had a Portuguese man o' war in my net. He must have left some venom in the bottom of the canoe. Sorry!"

And he should have been. A man o' war is a poisonous jellyfish that can kill you, and here I was sitting in a diluted solution of its secretion. It is a good thing I didn't have a date that evening. I was swollen, hurting, and wondering if my lower quarters were ever going to stop burning. They did, but from that day to this I have always given the man o' war a wide and respectful berth.

Chevy Pickup

On deck, we had a Chevy pickup truck for a coconut plantation owner on Little Corn Island east of the coast of Nicaragua. When we anchored out in the bay, the crew lowered the Chevy onto a lighter (A lighter is a small barge used to transport cargo to and from anchored ships. HPH III) and took it ashore. In those days, the 1930s, Corn Island was mostly coconut palms with a few houses clustered around each other to form sort of a settlement. Today, the 1980s, it is probably a bustling tourist trap full of neon signs, cocktail lounges, and bikinied New York stenographers. If it is, please don't tell me. I prefer the acres of lined-up coconut palms and the few tin-roofed houses.

We were there two days to load the nuts, and it only took those two days for the pickup to be de-fendered and dented so that it looked like a ten-year-old Mexican taxi. It still ran, as unbelievable as it seemed at the time. This was either a great living advertisement for General Motors or a huge compliment to the skillful mechanic who was on-the-job learning how to keep the new investment in working condition.

Doc

I was not especially proud of it, but I was still a virgin. The ship's doctor was a likable fellow but a rum pot whom Hollywood would have loved. He could be typecast as a drunken ship's doctor who was running away from it all. Doc spent his nondrinking time patching up split heads, repairing fight-damaged knuckles, and occasionally reviving a hungover workaway. Other times, he treated even less respectable problems such as crabs, clap, and threats of syphilis.

Serious venereal cases were treated ashore at a local hospital. By the time I had seen a few of those things, I was too scared to trade silk panties for services rendered. When I got back to high school that fall, it must have taken me a good two months before I worked up enough courage even to kiss my date good night.

I wonder what some of my school friends would have thought had they been with me to meet Sven's cousin?

Paint

Some of my Long Island boating friends like the following yarns.

One evening off the Jamaica coast, we got hit by a sudden squall that soon turned into a serious tropical storm. August isn't usually hurricane weather, but sometimes Mother Nature gets her calendar mixed up. That one was an off-season whopper.

The Old Man decided to run with it rather than swing around and pound into it. That was all right if he could keep the ship on course and prevent a broach. It was pretty exciting: black night, lightning, heavy seas, and the *Ringfond* bulling its bow into one big wave while another lifted its stern and shook the ship 'til she creaked like a couple of dozen rusty steel doors—which she mainly was.

The bo'sun had some men stringing lifelines, the mate had some others lashing down cargo to keep it from shifting, and the black gang built up a head of steam to keep up the forward speed. At the time, I was in the boiler room working a clinker bar. In between breaking up clinkers in the firebox with a fourteen-foot steel bar, which was my job at the time, I spent most of the watch trying to keep from being thrown against the hot boilers.

Some of us came up for air: 120 degrees in the fire room. We were soon very sorry we did, however. Down below, it was impossible to see the huge, white-topped seas rushing past the stern. Up here, cold, wet and dark, one had time to get scared. Then a large white-capped roller came along out of sequence and crashed over the lowered stern. Most of the water rushed over us and sloshed down the deck, but some of it slopped over the coaming into the open doorway and splashed into the hot engine room. (A coaming is a raised edge of a hatch to prevent water from sloshing in. HPH III).

During that storm, I developed a great respect for maritime paint. I was sure that the outer skin of uncountable layers of paint

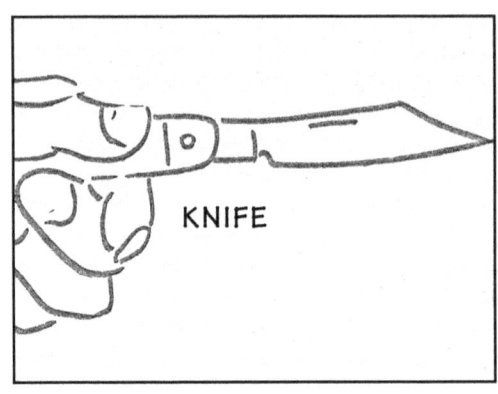

drawing by Peale during cruise on D/S Ringfond

held the ship together. From that day on, I treated her old rotted decks with proper awe and respect, never hitting her hard enough to really hurt, almost apologizing out loud if I did.

Knife

Nearly every sailor wears a knife. A sheath knife is as much a part of his work clothes as his pants or socks. One sunny afternoon, I sat on the forward hatch helping my friend carve a soft piece of wood. We got talking about knives, and he showed me a couple of good-sized scars. We then got talking about knife fighting, and the next thing I knew my friend was teaching me how to knife fight. Little did I know then that I would be wearing two knife scars before I quit the sea.

A knife fighter holds his weapon like a fencer holds his foil, blade pointed straight at his opponent, thumb on the top of the grip pointed along the blade. He crouches, snarls, dances, and jabs. No wild swings—just little short jabs. A really good knife fighter never bloodies his blade. If he yells, jabs, and raises a real ruckus, the other fellow will be half scared to death and depart the battlefield posthaste.

I forgot to ask what would happen if you picked on another real knife fighter who had planned to use the same tactic on you. A hasty retreat on your part would be called for, I imagine.

The two scars I wear resulted from, first, an unplanned, unexpected spontaneous reaction while a shipmate peeled potatoes and, second, a damned-fool mistake I made. Both to come later, and both while on the four-masted barque *Sea Cloud*.

Nonetheless, my little lesson on the *Ringfond* proved most valuable. First, I learned to respect, but not fear, a knife, and second, I learned what to do if someone should shove a knife in my face. I really believe his lesson saved, if not my life, at least a serious slash across the face. More about that later.

Beautiful Seamanship

In the Dominican Republic, the *Ringfond* entered such ports as Sanchez, a small trading port on the large bay called Bahia de Samana. There, we unloaded tins of paraffin that I learned later is the British way of saying coal, oil, or kerosene.

I saw some seamanship only a small steamer like *Ringfond* could get away with. Going upstream was no problem: pull up alongside the pier, make fast, and unload. But when it is time to leave, what do you do? The river is narrow, the current is strong, and there is little room to maneuver.

The skipper must have been there before. He headed upstream at quarter speed, barely the speed of the current. He then swung his bow gently into the bank on the port side. With the wheel in full hard-a-port, he signaled the engine room for full speed ahead. She creaked, she groaned, steam chuffed out of her safety valve, and the stern slowly swung upstream into the current with the bow acting as pivot. When the stern pointed well upstream, the captain had the quartermaster put the wheel hard over to full starboard and signaled the engine room to give him full astern. The *Ringfond* slowly backed upstream, the bow pulled away from the bank, and we were midstream ready to head out to sea. Rudder back to full port, engines half ahead, and there we were. A beautiful bit of seamanship!

At Santo Domingo, we tied up in a more routine manner. Not much excitement other than some gun fighting down around the central plaza. It was either the end, the beginning, or the middle of one of the ongoing revolutions that seemed to be the fashion at the time. We stayed near our ship, discharged whatever we should unload, and soon got underway once again.

Bucket of Bolts

drawing by Peale during cruise on D/S **Ringfond**

During that trip, another bit of my training hit home rather forcibly. One day, the bo'sun took me up to the paint locker, a small workshop in the forepeak. He gave me a metal pail half full of large bolts. Heavy as the devil, too. He said the engineer needed them down in the engine room and would I hop to it and get them to him as soon as possible. Off I went through the forward well deck, up the ladder, across the main deck, down another set of iron steps to the after well deck, up another steel stairway, and finally down into the after engine room. There, one of the wipers told me the chief had gone looking for the bucket of bolts, and I would find him up on the bridge. On the bridge, the mate told me I'd better shake a leg and get to the paint locker. He said the chief knew I had the bucket of bolts, and he had gone up to the paint locker to give me hell for having taken so long.

Down from the bridge, across the forward well deck, down into the paint locker I went—and no one was there. I hoped that the engine would hold together until I found the chief with the all-important bolts. So back to the engine room where the second told me I had just missed the chief. He said the chief was madder than hell and would skin me alive if I didn't get those bolts to him right away.

It was a two-handed job by that time. And also, by that time, I began to smell a rat, namely the bo'sun. I took the bucket, dumped the whole kaboodle over the side, and went to my bunk. Never heard another word.

Lesson #1054: Beware the bucket of bolts!

I have since recognized that practical joke in various disguises and so far haven't been caught a second time. First time could be an accident and the second time a coincidence, but the third time, pal, you have just been suckered.

Rum

In Kingston, Jamaica, I had time for a little sightseeing. I went to a sugar plantation and saw the whole process from crushing to burning to making brown sugar. Also, I went to a local rum refinery where, in the reception room, three faucets adorned the wall. One dispensed white rum, the second provided dark rum, and the third gave ice water. Right there I developed a taste for rum that lasted for many years until I tasted vodka in an underground bar in Leningrad, later Saint Petersburg. Never did I learn much about how rum is made.

Several years ago, I decided to collect photos of ships I have worked on. I finally found an organization that specializes in that sort of thing. They came up with information that, on her return to Oslo, *Ringfond* was sold, her name changed, and then sold again. She is probably on the bottom somewhere, having quietly sunk straight down when her paint finally gave way.

drawing by Peale during cruise on D/S Ringfond

George B. Cluett
of St. John's, Newfoundland
built in Tottensville, Staten Island, New York in 1911
length 135 feet • beam 26 feet • draft 12 feet
speed 6 knots under auxiliary power
June 15-September 14, 1934

The International Grenfell Association
INCORPORATED

SIR WILFRED GRENFELL, K.C.M.G., M.D.
EDWARD A. B. WILLMER, O.B.E., C.E.
EXECUTIVE OFFICER

SUPPORTING ASSOCIATIONS
GRENFELL ASSOCIATION OF AMERICA
NEW YORK, N.Y., U.S.A.
NEW ENGLAND GRENFELL ASSOCIATION
BOSTON, MASS., U.S.A.
GRENFELL LABRADOR MEDICAL MISSION
OTTAWA, CANADA
GRENFELL ASSOCIATION OF NEWFOUNDLAND
ST. JOHN'S, NEWFOUNDLAND
GRENFELL ASSOCIATION OF GREAT BRITAIN
AND IRELAND, LONDON, ENGLAND

156 FIFTH AVENUE, NEW YORK
TELEPHONE CHELSEA 3-1646

June 11, 1934

Mr. Peale Haldt,
"Birch Corners,"
Boonton, N. J.

Dear Mr. Haldt:

    The Staff Selection Committee of the International Grenfell Association takes great pleasure in giving you an appointment for the summer of 1934.

    A contract will soon be mailed to you for signature covering the period of service agreed upon, and designating the station and duty in which you are asked to serve. We feel that it is necessary to reserve the right to change the station to which you are designated if we find it advisable to do so.

    Please acknowledge the receipt of this letter of appointment.

Very sincerely yours,

Frederick E. Snyder

Frederick E. Snyder, Chairman,
Staff Selection Committee.

letter from the International Grenfell Association appointing Peale for the summer of 1934

International Grenfell Association, Inc.
156 Fifth Avenue, New York City

Copy

AGREEMENT made this 11th day of June, 19 34, between the INTERNATIONAL GRENFELL ASSOCIATION, INC., as Employer, and PEALE HALDT of "Birch Corners," Boonton, New Jersey, as Employee.

The Employee agrees to serve the Employer in the capacity of Seaman upon the following terms:

1. The service shall extend for a period of 3 months commencing June 15, 1934, and ending Sept. 14, 1934.

   (These dates shall indicate the dates of departure from and return to the home country or the country of residence of the Employee, and can only be approximate owing to the uncertainties of travel. Prolongation or curtailment of this period is subject to agreement between Employer and Employee.)

2. Such service shall be given by the Employee as a free gift to the Employer without pay.

3. The Employee shall be stationed at "Cluett" or at such other place as the Employer may determine.

4. During the employment under this agreement the Employee shall give his or her entire time to the duties of the position, and shall obey the rules and regulations of the Association.

5. In case of prolonged illness the Employer may cancel employment at his option.

6. If the Employee shall be guilty of misconduct or shall refuse to obey any reasonable order, the Employer may cancel this agreement upon notice.

7. While the Employee is at his or her station, the Employer shall be represented in all negotiations with the Employee by the Medical Officer in charge of the District. Only in case the Employee desires to appeal from the decision of the Medical Officer in charge of the District shall the Employee communicate directly with the Employer. Appeals should be addressed to the Chairman of the Staff Selection Committee.

8. The Employer does not assume responsibility for the life or health of those in the service of the Association.

9. This agreement shall be deemed made in Newfoundland, and shall be so construed.

10. The following special conditions are incorporated herein:

    All expenses of travel and maintenance shall be borne by the Employee.

INTERNATIONAL GRENFELL ASSOCIATION, INC.

Witness *Grace V. Euart* by *H. Snyder*
Witness *Edward R. Klemm* *Peale Haldt*

(Blue Sheet—Non-salaried staff member who pays all expenses. Original to the Chairman, Staff Selection Committee, duplicate to the Employee and triplicate to the Medical Officer in charge of the District)

contract from the International Grenfell Association for Peale for the summer of 1934

The International Grenfell Association
INCORPORATED
SIR WILFRED GRENFELL, K.C.M.G., M.D.
EDWARD A. B. WILLMER, O.B.E., C.E.
EXECUTIVE OFFICER

SUPPORTING ASSOCIATIONS
GRENFELL ASSOCIATION OF AMERICA
NEW YORK, N.Y., U.S.A.
NEW ENGLAND GRENFELL ASSOCIATION
BOSTON, MASS., U.S.A.
GRENFELL LABRADOR MEDICAL MISSION
OTTAWA, CANADA
GRENFELL ASSOCIATION OF NEWFOUNDLAND
ST. JOHN'S, NEWFOUNDLAND
GRENFELL ASSOCIATION OF GREAT BRITAIN
AND IRELAND, LONDON, ENGLAND

156 FIFTH AVENUE, NEW YORK
TELEPHONE CHELSEA 3-1646

June 11, 1934

Mr. Peale Haldt, "Birch Corners," Boonton, N. J.

Dear Mr. Haldt:

The CLUETT will sail from Maine State Pier, Portland, Maine, on June 21, 1934. Will you please report on board to Captain Kenneth Iversen during the forenoon of that date.

You will be asked to pay for your board while serving on the CLUETT at the rate of $1.00 a day. We should be very much obliged to you if you will make prepayment for board by sending us a check for $100.00 before you sail. Adjustment will be made at the end of the summer if the cost of your board is more or less than this amount.

Very sincerely yours,

F. E. Shnyder, Chairman,
Staff Selection Committee.

FES/E

instructions from the International Grenfell Association for Peale about where to report to the George B. Cluett as a seaman

*cover of the log book kept by Peale during
his summer working aboard George B. Cluett with sample log entry on the next page
• transcriptions begin on page 155 •*

Sunday 22nd 10:00 P.M.

A lot of excitement today. We all put on the glad rags, piled into a dory and headed for the church. The only church here and the minister was away so we headed for the opposite shore to the mission. There we stayed until noon, talking and reading. After dinner some went ashore but two of us stayed on board and read. I slept a bit, too. At 4 am o'clock we rowed ashore just in time to see the sandwich plate empty. We did get a cookie or two and a splash of tea. I came back and climbed up in the topmast head to read. From the [smell?] that [you'd?] think it was rum or something I had instead of tea. I was reading the Strand Magazine, printed in England. Tom and I got our dinner tonight. We had toasted cheese sandwiches, fried spuds, etc. After dinner I was oft reading some of the skipper's books when we decided to go up in the airplane. It costs $2.50 for 15 minutes. 6 guys - on the skipper, all flew for about 15 minutes. At one time we were 2,500 ft. high and at another time we hit 130 M.P.H. It was a Fairchild seaplane owned by the Canadian Airways Limited. The only trouble is Jim broke now and won't be able to buy that eskimo dickie. Hope there's some kale at St. Anthone.

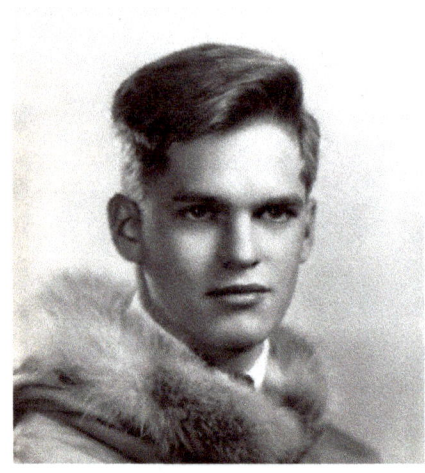

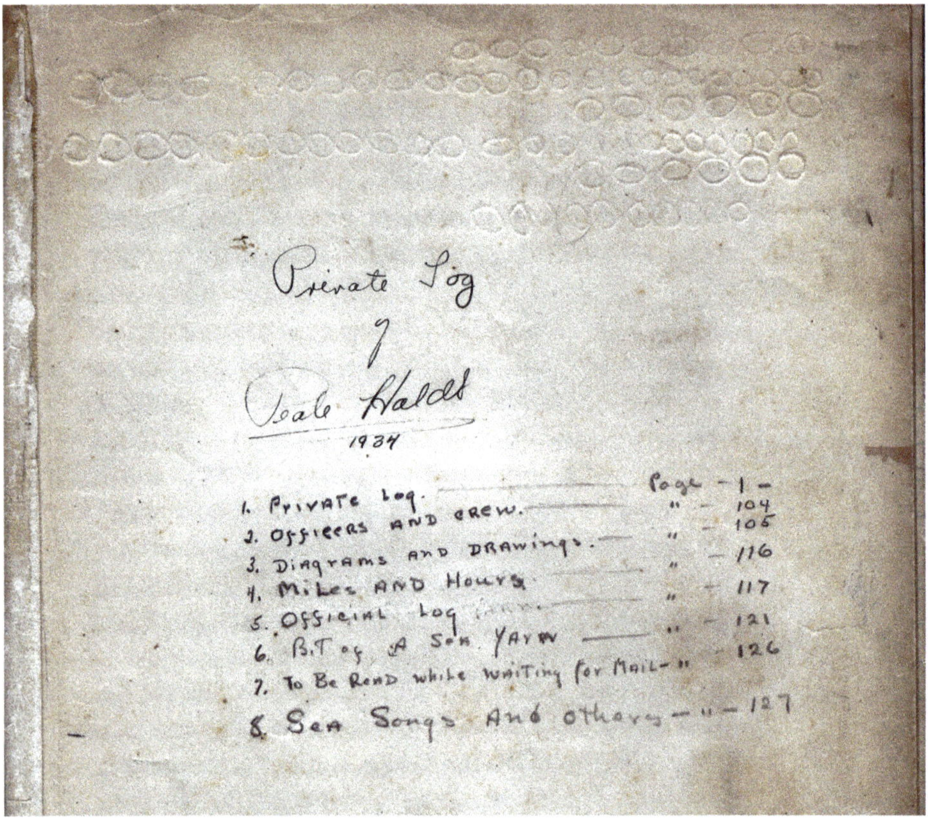

Private Log
of
Peale Haldt
1934

1. Private Log. — Page - 1 -
2. Officers and Crew. — " - 104
3. Diagrams and Drawings. — " - 105
4. Miles and Hours — " - 116
5. Official Log — " - 117
6. B.T of A Sea Yarn — " - 121
7. To Be Read while waiting for Mail - " - 126
8. Sea Songs And others - " - 127

Peale, top, at seventeen; the inside cover of the log book he kept during his summer working aboard the George B. Cluett

• transcriptions begin on page 155 •

George B. Cluett, *right, next to a supply ship in dock*

George B. Cluett

The Grenfell Association was headquartered in St. Anthony, a small coastal village on Hare Bay, the northernmost tip of Newfoundland. Started by Sir Wilfred Grenfell, the association consisted of a string of hospitals along the Labrador coast. The hospitals were the only places native Eskimos, Indian, French, and various cross breeds could go for medical attention. Sir Wilfred's books, such as *The Labrador Doctor* and *Adrift on an Ice Pan*, paint a picture of unbearable hardships that prompted that young British doctor to chuck a life of comfort and go to Labrador to take care of local natives. In the summer, they were mostly fishermen and trappers. In the long, cold winters, they merely tried to stay alive. I am sure that the air base at Goose Bay, the hydroelectric power plants and ore mines have changed all that, but back in 1934, it remained wild, desolate, and beautiful country.

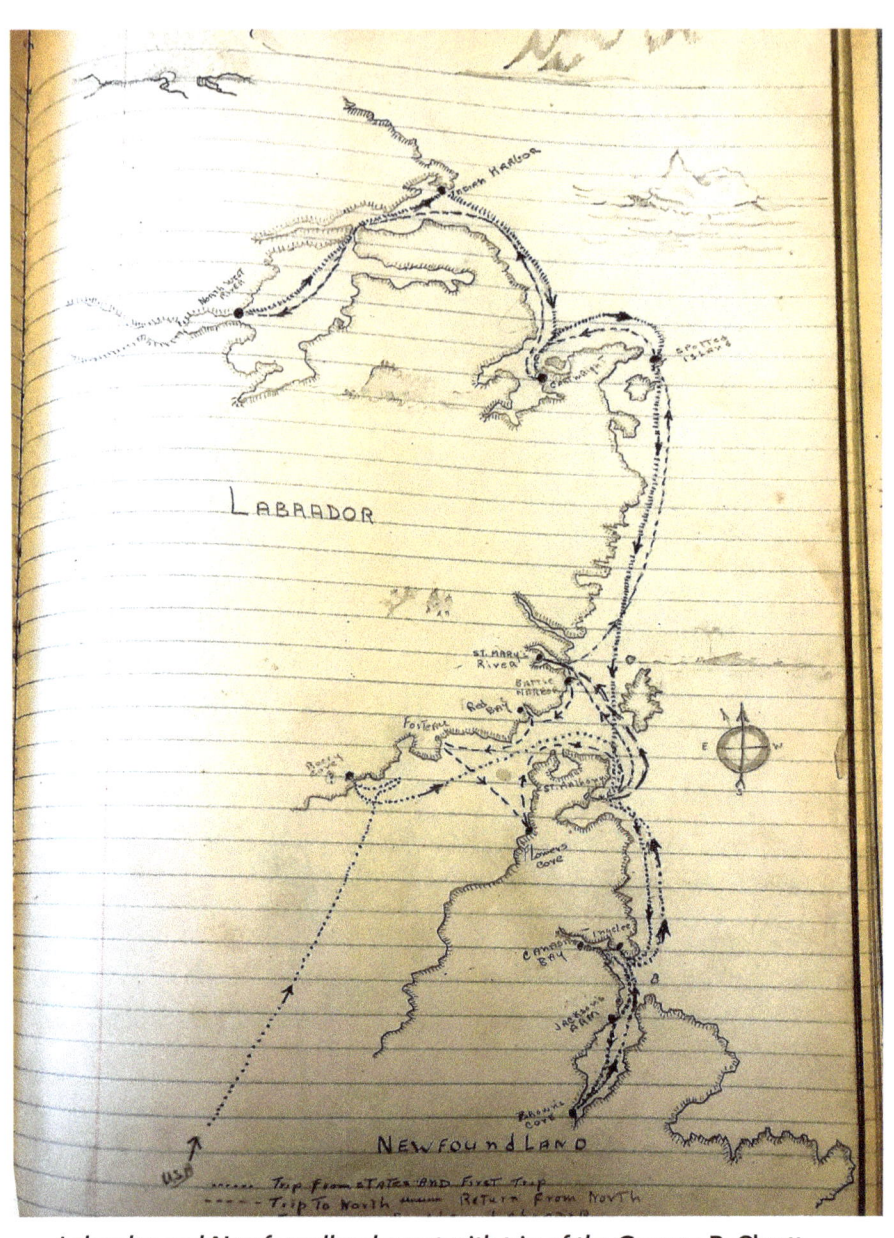

Labrador and Newfoundland coast with trip of the George B. Cluett drawing by Peale from his 1934 log aboard the Cluett

The association also owned a ship used to haul supplies to hospitals located at such far removed places as Northwest River, Indian Harbor, and Cartwright, to name a few. This vessel, the *George B. Cluett*, was a converted Grand Banks fisherman captained by a Blue Nose, or a seadog who has crossed the Arctic Circle, from Lunenberg, Nova Scotia. She had a Viking-like, square rigged foresail, a fore staysail, jib, and a huge mainsail. The skipper was Captain P. K. Iverson, and with initials like that, he was soon christened "Chicklets," a term of endearment used only when he was out of hearing distance.

We also had a 225-pound cook whose real name we never knew. He was Cookie, as far as we were concerned. His name may be lost but his picturesque language will never fade. In the fo'c'sle, he had an old coal stove that never went out. It always had something steaming away on it, the pots held in place by movable iron rods. On it, Cookie produced nourishing, filling, and distinctive meals. They even tasted good and all hands accepted them as long as we didn't ask too many questions about the ancestry of the mysterious ingredients.

WOP

The entire crew consisted of a professional captain, a chief engineer, and our beloved cook along with six WOPS. I was a WOP. The term has nothing to do with ethnic background. Rather, it means we signed on without pay. The hospital system worked the same way—a bunch of professional doctors and nurses and a whole passel of nurses-in-training, nurses aides, and future doctors all willing to gain experience while enjoying the unusual. Eat raw blubber if you wish, watch the silent curtain of the Aurora Borealis sweep across the night sky, jig for cod for dinner that evening, and listen to the Indians tell of their trapping experiences. Nothing like that in the Rockaway River Hospital in Boonton, New Jersey, or the Northern Westchester Hospital in Mount Kisco, New York. (two of the towns my father lived in early and later in his life, HPH III)

Diving Exhibition

At Cartwright, we were to unload a deck cargo of coal. Four banjo wielders (and anyone who ever was a coal passer does not have to be told that the big, heavy, wide-bladed coal scoops are banjos), including me, stripped to the waist shoveling two tons of coal onto the dock where shore-based WOPS wheelbarrowed it up to the hospital building a few hundred yards up the hill. We were sweating, and coal dust covered us from head to foot. A little old lady, a tourist from St. Anthony, watched us and was somewhat surprised to learn when we wiped our faces that we were Caucasians. She reminded us that it was Sunday and hadn't we better get finished so we could go to chapel. We looked at each other, each of us looking more like Al Jolson than ourselves, grinned, and said that we didn't have any clean clothes. She laid into us with such determination that it was easier to say OK than fight her off. The clincher came when she said, "God doesn't care what you look like, why should you?" That evening we kept our promise. She wasn't there.

When we finished shoveling the coal, we went below, grabbed some soap, stripped ourselves naked, climbed back on deck, and dived overboard. The water was really cold, but it didn't bother us. We washed and proceeded to put on a diving exhibition doing one-and-a-halfs, somersaults, swans, backjacks, and pikes. We even climbed part way up the

the crew of the George B. Cluett *with Peale, shirtless, right, second from front*

rigging to add height for the more spectacular dives. In no time at all, a crowd had gathered around our vessel. The men sat in kayaks, rowboats, and small fishing boats. Turned out that natives don't swim up there—too damned cold, and they are too damned smart.

With an attentive audience, we really put on a show. We were blue with cold, but our appreciative audience clapped and hollered so much that we wouldn't quit. Only then did one of us notice that a number of the well-bundled audience were girls—Indian girls, Eskimo girls, and Grenfell girls from the local nursing staff. Our swimming uniform was totally us, blue and goose bumped, but just us. We wondered whether cheering and clapping was for our diving or for our exposed manliness.

On the way back after the show, I stepped on the top flat rung of the eight-inch vertical ladder that led down to the fo'c'sle, and there lay a cake of soap. I thumped down the hatch, cracking my head in the process, and found that I had landed spank in the middle of a coffee klatch presided over by Cookie and attended by visiting Grenfell nurses. And there I was naked as a jay bird, flat on my back, and half unconscious to boot. I came to with my head in a nurse's lap and a large bandage on the back of my head.

Couldn't have picked a better place to split my head open. Then some wiseacre

Peale's log account of hitting his head • transcriptions begin on page 155 •

had to spoil it all by saying, "It's a good thing you landed on your head. A fall like that would have killed anyone else." At this point, I usually let my listeners feel the lump on the back of my head, said lump being accompanied by a second one a little lower down that came several years later in Keil, Germany, when some of Hitler's Brown Shirts took exception to something one of my shipmates said. More on that later.

Survey Plane

One day, a Canadian survey plane put its pontoons down close by the *Cluett*. A couple of us talked the pilot into exchanging a cup of Cookie's coffee for a ride in his plane. Then we talked our skipper into joining us. He had never been up in a plane before, so we had to give him a lot of credit for even getting into the cramped cabin, let alone agreeing to go aloft.

Once we were airborne, it was quite a thrill looking down on all of the huge cliffs of rocks that make up the coastline of Labrador. The biggest thrill for all of us was to hear our captain say, "Lord, I've been sailing these waters for over thirty years. I know every channel, every ledge, and every crosscurrent down the coast but never have I seen it so clear and plain as I do now." And he was right. From a thousand feet, you could see deep into the

customer copy of Canadian Airways Limited passenger ticket Peale signed for observation flight with other Cluett *crew members, including Captain Iverson*

clear water and find great underwater rocks and ledges that up until then had been merely lines on a chart.

Skip never forgot that ride. I only hope that he had the opportunity to see more of his beloved coast before he died.

Sir Wilfred

One evening, I had the distinct privilege of being invited to the Grenfell home in St. Anthony. Sir Wilfred (we noticed that Lady Grenfell called him Wil) served us coffee and cookies and, with only a little prompting, had us in a circle at his feet while

Peale turns eighteen
• transcriptions begin on page 155 •

he told story after story about his adventures along the coast. One story in particular bears repeating. For others, look up some of his books. I will guarantee you they are real spellbinders.

One winter, an Eskimo seal fisherman gave himself a nasty cut on his hand when he pulled the barbed spear out of a dead seal. As time progressed, the slash became infected. He knew that the hospital was weeks away through miles of subzero wilderness and he also knew he had to do something about it right away. So, with his heavy hunting blade he severed his hand at the wrist, wrapped a tourniquet around his arm, and stuck the stub into a container of flour. In time, it cauterized itself and healed perfectly. So perfectly, said Sir Wilfred, that when he made his spring tour and saw the healed stump, he asked the native the name of the surgeon who had amputated the hand. Sir Wilfred was thoroughly amazed when he heard what had happened.

Sir Wilfred told his stories, but he had one bad habit that drove us crazy. He got to the exciting part, interrupted himself, and when he was ready to start again, he forgot where he had left off. That evening at his home, Lady Grenfell saved us from returning to our ship with half a dozen unfinished stories. She politely and patiently reminded him where he had stopped. He then finished each of his tales much to our relief and satisfaction.

One day while we were loading supplies to go down the coast, Sir Wilfred came alongside in his sealskin hunting kayak. The true Eskimo kayak is light, strong, and fast, especially made to help the hunter skim quietly over the water to get within range of his unsuspecting quarry. Sir Wilfred was as dexterous as any Eskimo and better than most. We challenged him to a race, us on foot and him in his kayak, from one end of the pier to the other. That was a bad mistake. We ran as fast as we could (and I was a quarter-miler on my track team back home), but he was sitting there in his motionless kayak waiting for us at the end of the race.

Wilfred T. Grenfell, MD, from **The Story of Grenfell of the Labrador** *by Dillon Wallace, 1922*

Our Girl

We all had one sweetheart at the Headquarters Hospital in St. Anthony. I don't remember her name, but I do recall she came from New Jersey, my home state. Whenever our ship was due in to pick up supplies, she met us and usually had a fresh cake or some other goodie for us six WOPS to divvy up. She loved us all, and we all equally loved her. When we visited with her, we all accompanied each other—one big happy family you might say. One day we got a wireless message that our girl was dead. We asked the skipper if we could please go back to St. Anthony in time to attend her funeral. He knew how we felt about her, so he changed plans to get us there on time.

Up in the local cemetery on the north side of the harbor, a grave had been dug in the rocky hillside. The six of us lowered her casket and turned away as the rocky soil thudded down on the plain wooden casket. It was not until sometime later that we heard she had taken her own life rather than go home pregnant. We knew for a fact that no one from the *Cluett* was the father simply because we were always together the few times we were with her. It's just as well that we never heard who impregnated her, because I am sure we would have beaten him to a bloody pulp. I have since heard that her family had her remains brought back to New Jersey. Too bad in a way—that lonely, windy knoll in St. Anthony is where we remember her.

Indian Tickle

Indian Tickle is the entrance to a rockbound fishing harbor where the settlement bore the obvious name of Indian Harbor.

schooner **George B. Cluett** *at Indian Tickle, Labrador*

Our skipper explained that a tickle is any rock-surrounded, narrow passage just barely wide enough to maneuver through. When pressed, he said he really didn't know where the word came from except that it is "damned ticklish" to sail through some of those passages. After that airplane trip I told you about, even the captain was surprised that he had sailed through some of them.

Cookie

Our cookie was quite a character. Not only did he concoct meals out of nowhere, but he also had two special kettles on the back of the galley stove. One contained what he called coffee and the other he insisted was tea. Both liquids were thick, black, and guaranteed to warm up a body as long as it was still alive. The contents of either pot also guaranteed that the drinker would be wide awake during his four-hour watch and maybe for some time after that if one managed to swallow more than one cupful. Only by smell could we tell which was which. If you wanted coffee and got tea, you could arrange to swap with someone who had made the mistake in reverse. Also, if you added a lot of sugar and tinned milk, you could accept it as a drink of pleasure rather than a drink of necessity.

crew on board **Cluett** *with Peale at right*

Watching Cookie make the stuff was unbelievable, and it could make a water drinker out of you if you weren't careful. He would take a handful of coffee he had just ground and dump it into one pot. Tea leaves he would dump into the other pot. Never did any of us see him mix up the procedure, although I am not sure we could have told the difference if he had. We learned to love the damned stuff, and we considered anyone a sissy who couldn't down a cup or two at one sitting. When one of his pots got half full of grounds or leaves, he simply dumped it over the side and started all over again.

Dog Basket

The skipper ate alone back in his own cabin. Cookie had a double-decked wooden tray or box he called a dog basket for some reason. He had cut holes in the upper deck of the box so it could hold plates, a cup, a glass, and eating utensils as well as a napkin. A napkin? By God, our Old Man ate in style, I'll tell you. Every mealtime, the dog basket was loaded, and Cookie pulled his chef's hat down around his ears. He carried the dog basket across the windswept deck back to the skipper. He would be muttering to himself about goddamned this, bastardly that, and f***ing something else, all the while putting plates of food down on our table so we could eat, too. Our skipper was no Captain Bligh. He ate the same things we ate. It's just that he had it served better—and used a napkin!

This one dark night, we were bucking a storm, and water was washing green over the rail and sloshing around on deck. Cookie prepared the muttered-over dog basket, jammed down his chef's hat again, climbed up the vertical ladder, and went out onto the swaying deck. In a moment, we heard a loud crash, an unmistakable sound of shattered crockery ,and the metallic clang of thrown knives, forks, and spoons. Knowing Cookie as we did, we waited—and, sure enough, it happened. First, and to this day I swear it's true, the seas seemed to calm down a little. Next, the ship seemed to level off a bit, and even the wind died down somewhat. It got ominously quiet—and then it hit! We rushed out on deck to see if our cook was still on board, and there he was, all 225 pounds of him, apron flapping in the wind, arms raised above his head and clenched fists shaken heavenward.

Cookie stood there bellowing to Jesus on a one-to-one basis, "Come down, come down you blue-balled son-of-a-bitch, you

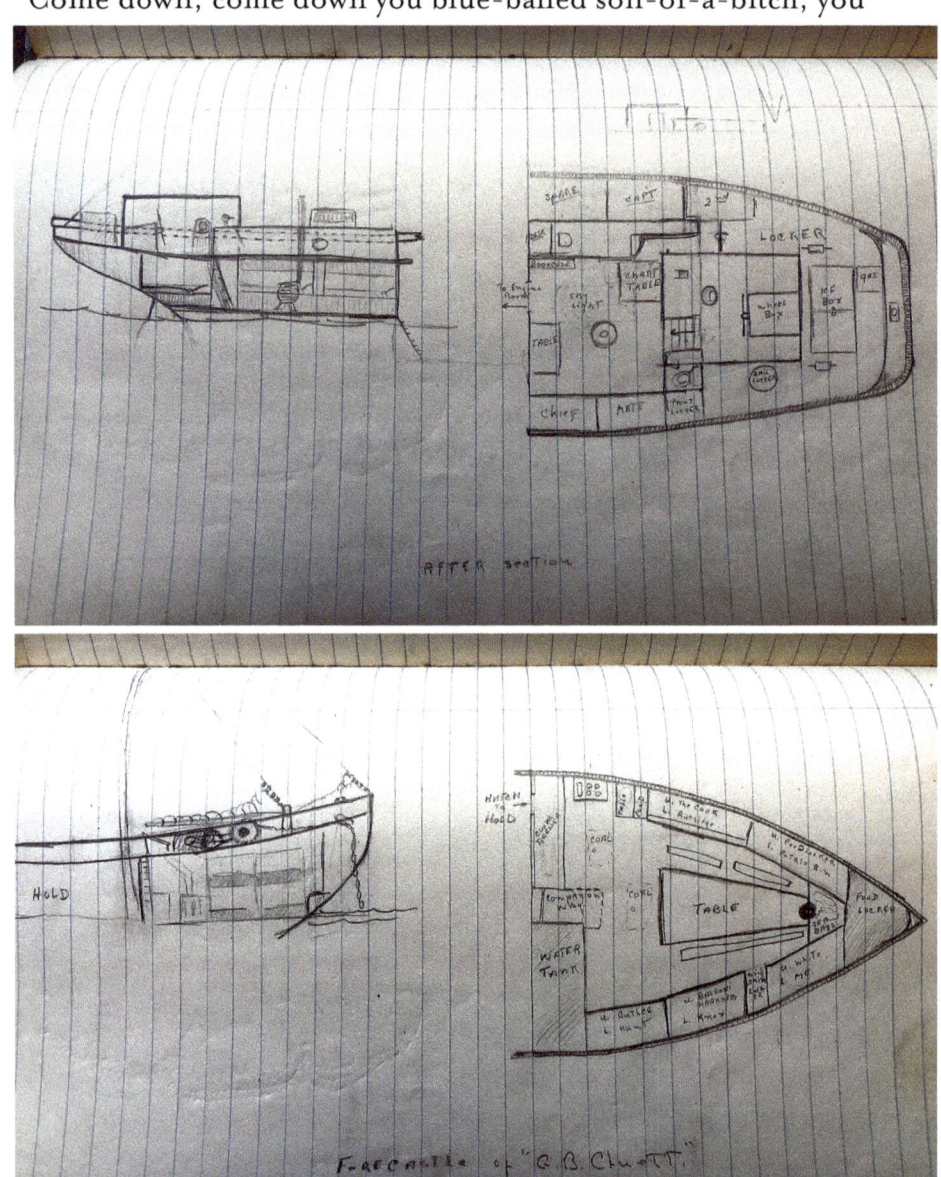

Peale's drawing of Cluett aft section, top
Peale's drawing of Cluett full plan, bottom

Peale's taking things into his own hands in his log after receiving no postal mail in days before internet, wifi, texting, smart phones when only postal mail or telegrams provided correspondence

snot-nosed son of unmarried Mary. Come down, and I'll pound you into little piles of balled up ****. I'll shove every ****ing thing down your ****ing throat!!"

We had always been proud of our cookie. He could outfight, outdrink, outswear any man living, dead, or yet-to-be-born, but that was his lifetime masterpiece. We were transfixed, afraid to move. He was redfaced and so close to frothing at the mouth that we were afraid he might throw two or three of us overboard as he thought of more challenges to hurl at our Lord. To this day I never understood why we didn't glow like a halo, get struck by a bolt of lightning, and sink without a trace.

All I can say even now is that we have a very patient Lord and Master watching over us.

Pack Ice

One evening, a shipmate and I were lolling on the forward hatch watching the sun go down when we noticed that we were coming up on a few chunks of flat pack ice. Because of a canvas-covered deck cargo, it was difficult for the man at the wheel to see the surface of the water. We were not sure that the helmsman could see the ice, so we called back to him in a rather unseaman-like manner to "watch out for the ice" or something to that effect. The Old Man came roaring out of the wheel house, climbed over the deck cargo, and saw us loafing around sightseeing. Somehow or other, somebody had gotten something mixed up, and there was no bow watch (which was supposed to be me) on duty.

I don't remember why. I probably thought the other fellow was on bow watch, and he probably thought I was. Either way, there had been no lookout on duty all the time we were there.

First, the skipper got us through the ice without a rerun of the Titanic episode, and then he came back to blister us. He wasn't in the same league, let alone the same ballpark as our cookie, so his cussing landed on deaf ears already well calloused by Cookie's unchallenged proficiency. Anyhow, in no time at all there was a man on bow watch. One clang on the bow bell if we sighted ice to port, two clangs if to starboard and, if the ice were dead ahead, a solid clatter of clangs, the nearer the ice the more frantic the ringing.

A few days later I was on bow watch again. That time I knew it, and I was alert to all danger. Off on the port horizon floated a small berg. One clang of the bell. Out popped the skipper.

"Where?"

"There, off on the horizon about ten degrees" I said.

The Old Man squinted his eyes, stared out to the horizon, looked at me, looked at the iceberg about ten miles away, turned on his heels, and muttered something about "goddamned farmers" as he walked away.

Well, what the hell? We didn't have icebergs down in the Caribbean!

Another lesson learned.

Knife fights. I have a scar on my left hand from a little to-do on the *Sea Cloud* that I will tell you about later. We darned near had one on the *Cluett*, too, over something just as meaningless. Living in close quarters day in and day out does something to you. No privacy, no place to be alone. A very different way of life indeed.

Labradorite

You may know labradorite, a glassy bluish mineral in the feldspar family, as a beautiful gemstone. Large crystals show a glowing display of colors reminiscent of gasoline spilled on water. When polished, the crystals make wonderful bookends, paperweights, and conversation pieces.

We bought several beautiful pieces in the St. Anthony headquarters. The crystals are sensitive to sudden shocks and shatter when dropped. During all the moves our family has made since I came ashore, I am afraid I have misplaced my one unbroken specimen.

Aloft

Our unique square sail on the foremast was unfurled whenever we had a following wind. We worked on a pair of Fairbanks Morse diesels that the engineer started by dropping a lighted cigarette into the cylinder. I don't really know how that worked, but it never failed. The forestays'l and jib would be set if the wind came off the after quarter and, if the wind was just right, we would unfurl the big main. As an off-duty pleasure on a bright, sunny day we would walk out on the boom and lean back into the belly of the filled mainsail. It was often possible to get well beyond the deck and look straight down at the creamy seas thrown back by the curling bow wave. I never did understand why the skipper let us do that. Guess he figured if we fell off it was our own damn fault in the first place, we could swim in the second place, and, if worst came to worst, we could grab hold of the log line always towed astern and holler for help in the third place.

A taut wire about as thick around as the ends of your three middle fingers stretched between the foremast and main right near where the topmasts fit onto the telephone-pole-sized lower masts. Other wire cable extended from the foremast down to the bow, and other cables

Peale (in a photo that missed the top of his head) atop the Cluett *main mast*

stretched astern and down the sides. All that standing rigging braced the masts against the roughest seas and strongest wind.

I was looking aloft at that rigging when I recalled one of my dad's tales. As I remembered, he climbed the main to the break and went hand-over-hand to the foremast. It would be like climbing out of the attic window and swinging out to a tree about thirty feet away. I looked it over, decided if he could do it so could his son, and so up I went and across I went.

The skipper came out on deck, looked up, and saw me when I was about halfway out. What he said could be summarized into a pithy sentence: "Get the hell down out of there, you damned fool!"

I wasn't about to let go at thirty-five or forty feet up, so I continued across, came down, and got blistered some more by an irate captain. To make matters worse, when I got home and told all of my stories to my family, this one didn't go over very well. Seems I had misheard something, because Dad said he never actually

Peale, left, with another crew member on the Cluett *spreader*

climbed from one mast to the other—he had just thought about it. So I got blistered again!

Charlie North

I was introduced to Charlie North on that trip. Charlie North, it seems, has shipped out on every sailing ship from the clipper days through the days of the whalers right down to the present. Only I didn't know it. The captain, the cookie, and the engineer had us going until one of them spilled the beans. Charlie North is the name given to the black stovepipe with its cone-shaped top that sticks out through the galley roof. Try that one out on some of your yachting friends. Two will get you five that darned few ever met Charlie.

When the trip ended, the fall season was well on its way. In fact, school had started and I got there a bit late. I had enrolled in Perkiomen Prep in Pennsburg, Pennsylvania, where I would have a bunch of Latin crammed into me so I could pass certain college entrance exams. When I arrived there, I learned the others had given me the nickname Eskimo. My roommate explained that, when he arrived to find a missing roomie, the dean told him not to worry, he would have his roommate. It was just that the missing roommate would arrive a little late from Labrador!

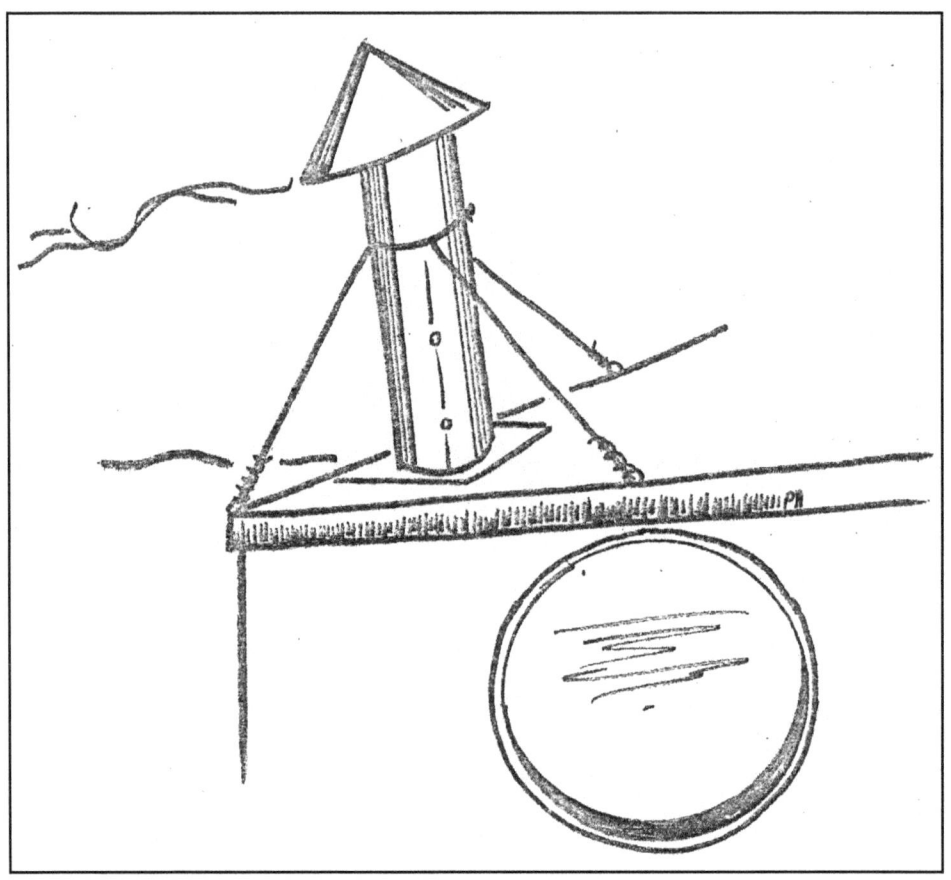

Peale's drawing of Charlie North, the Cluett *galley stovepipe*

The International Grenfell Association
INCORPORATED
SIR WILFRED GRENFELL, K.C.M.G., M.D.
EDWARD A. B. WILLMER, O.B.E., C.E.
EXECUTIVE OFFICER

SUPPORTING ASSOCIATIONS
GRENFELL ASSOCIATION OF AMERICA
NEW YORK, N.Y., U.S.A.
NEW ENGLAND GRENFELL ASSOCIATION
BOSTON, MASS., U.S.A.
GRENFELL LABRADOR MEDICAL MISSION
OTTAWA, CANADA
GRENFELL ASSOCIATION OF NEWFOUNDLAND
ST. JOHN'S, NEWFOUNDLAND
GRENFELL ASSOCIATION OF GREAT BRITAIN
AND IRELAND, LONDON, ENGLAND

156 FIFTH AVENUE, NEW YORK
TELEPHONE CHELSEA 3-1646

Oct. 18, 1934

Mr. Peale Haldt,
"Birch Corners,"
Boonton, N. J.

Dear Mr. Haldt:

Having heard that you have reached this country from the North, I am writing to express our sincere appreciation for the service you have rendered during the past summer. I trust you have found many satisfactions in giving this service. We have received great benefit.

Very sincerely yours,

F. E. Shnyder, Chairman,
Staff Selection Committee.

FES/E

a thank you to Peale from the International Grenfell Association acknowledging his service on the Cluett

Sea Cloud
of Jacksonville, Florida
built in Kiel, Germany, in 1931
length 316 feet • beam 49 feet • draft 16 feet
speed 12 knots under auxiliary power
April 27-July 30, 1937

on board Jacksonville, Fla.
March 26, 1937

Aux. Barque "Sea Cloud"
P.O. Box 1151, Jacksonville, Fla.

H. Peale Haldt Jr.,
Theta Chi Fraternity,
Hamilton, N.Y.

My Dear Mr. Haldt:-

    Your letter of March 15th I received some time ago. I have lately received orders from the owners to fit the ship out for a trip to Europe, and I expect to be in New York with the ship around April 20th.

    I suppose you are posted with the new shipping laws which large yachts have to comply with the same as passenger ships, that is, we have to carry licensed officers, and all A.B. seamen have to have Continuous Discharge Books, as well as A.B. and Lifeboat certificates. Ordinary seamen have to have the Discharge books and O. S. and Lifeboat certificates, so for you to join this ship you must have the Continuous Discharge Book and either A.B. or O.S. certificate as well as the Lifeboat certificate. Let me know as soon as you get the book and certificates, which you can get in New York from the U.S. Local Inspectors, and I'll keep a berth open for you, either as A.B. or O.S.

    I don't know how long our trip will be this time. Hoping to hear from you no later than April 15th, address mail to me here in Jacksonville.

    Yours very truly,

C. W. Lawson,
Master, Yacht SEA CLOUD

letter of March 26, 1937, to Peale from Captain C. W. Lawson, master, yacht Sea Cloud explaining qualifications to become a member of the crew

MARJORIE POST DAVIES
POSTUM BUILDING
250 PARK AVENUE
NEW YORK CITY

March 2, 1937

Mr. H. Peale Holdt, Jr.
Theta Chi House
Colgate University
Hamilton, New York

My dear Mr. Holdt:

Acknowledging your letter of February 19th, I would suggest that you communicate with Captain Lawson. His address is:

c/o Yacht Sea Cloud
P. O. Box 1151
Jacksonville, Florida

While we have had no definite instructions, I believe that the Sea Cloud will sail for European waters by the first of May or thereabouts. It would, therefor, seem to me rather early for you to get away from college, even if Captain Lawson could use you.

Furthermore, I wonder if you realize that it is pretty hard work on board the yacht. Just because she is a private pleasure craft does not mean that there are any soft snaps. Captain Lawson demands hard work from his crew. However, you can write him if you feel inclined.

Yours very truly,

William R. Wood

WRW:CF

letter of March 2, 1937, from William R. Wood, representative of Marjorie Post Davies, to Peale giving address and initial sailing plan for Sea Cloud as well as thoughts about timing and hard work on board as a prospective member of the crew

March 15, 1937

Captain C.W. Lawson
c/o Yacht Sea Cloud
Jacksonville, Florida

Sir:

Recently a communication from Mr. W.R. Wood arrived in which he advised me to get in immediate touch with you concerning a berth on the "Sea Cloud" this summer.

I realize that the work on a private yacht must be on a higher level of efficiency than on the trading schooner and the freighters I have worked on and realize your position depends on the care with which this work is accomplished. I feel, however, that the experiences I shall gain would far outweigh the necessary efforts.

The regrettable experience of last summer----the mishandling of belated mails at the University---shall not recur this season. I understand an early sailing date will be necessitated. If the opportunity is again open for me, would it be possible to mention an approximate date? With this knowledge it might be arranged for me to leave the University at an earlier period.

Respectfully,

H. Peale Haldt jr.

letter of March 15, 1937, from Peale to Captain Lawson indicating his desire to work on board Sea Cloud *that summer*

Iota Chapter
Theta Chi Fraternity
Hamilton, N. Y.

Approved by this Committee — *April 9, 1937*

April 9, 1937

Committee of Petitions
Administration Building
Colgate University

PETITION OF PEALE HALDT '39

Gentlemen:

This summer Ambassador Davies, United States envoy to Russia, will sail from New York to the Coronation on his yacht, "Sea Cloud". There he will entertain royal guests and review the Royal Naval manoeuvers at Spithead. After the festivities the yacht will cruise across the North Sea to Leningrad---- the first great yacht to make the port since it was Petrograd.

Thru efforts of certain officials and after a direct correspondence with Captain C.W. Lawson, master of the yacht, it is now possible for me to ship on board her for the summer as Ordinary Seaman. I have in my possession the required certificates of service and other needed credentials. The experience necessary for such a trip has been gained on board freighters, a fishing trawler, and on Sir Wilfred Grenfell's schooner, the "George B. Cluett". My parents are very much in favor of the plan and have given me full permission to go.

Unfortunately this necessitates leaving about May 1st. I have spoken to my professors and they have endorsed the plan with their individual consent stating that I could make up the work missed. I have been advised that I should write a petition in the hopes that some adjustment can be arranged to make it possible for me to leave before the end of the college year.

Enclosed are the letters, papers, and certificates referred to.

Respectfully yours,

Peale Haldt

P.S. Would it be at all possible to inform me before Sunday night as Capt. Lawson must have my reply before leaving Florida, about April 12th.

Peale's petition of April 9, 1937, to Colgate University, requesting "some adjustment" to leave school about May 1 to ship on board Sea Cloud *for the summer and approved the same day*

Aux. Barque "Sea Cloud"
P.O. Box 1151, Jacksonville, Fla.

on board Jacksonville, Fla.
April 12th 1937

H. Peale Haldt Jr.,
Theta Chi Fraternity,
Hamilton, N.Y.

My Dear Mr. Haldt:-

Your telegram received. I will have a berth open for you as Ordinary Seaman. You join the SEA CLOUD at City Island, N.Y., April 26th.

Proceed from New York City to Anderson's Gasoline Dock, City Island where you will find a launch from the SEA CLOUD connecting every half hour. Do not bring any trunk with you. You will be furnished with uniforms, working clothes, boots, rain clothes etc. You have to furnish your own underwear, socks, also your civilian clothes.

While you are in New York, try to get your Life Boat Certificate, if you have not already got one. I understand you have your O.S. endorsement and your Continuous Discharge Book.

Hoping to see you on board April 26th.

Yours very truly,

C. W. Lawson,
Master, Yacht SEA CLOUD

"I will have a berth open for you as Ordinary Seaman," in letter from Captain Lawson to Peale on April 12, 1937

15

Thursday June 11th

Several days ago we were in Kiel. There we were to go into dry dock and have our bottom (the ship, of course) scraped. The dock broke down and so we had to sail for Stettin where a larger dock could be obtained. Kiel is too Navy minded. Every body either has a uniform or they are women. All the ship yards have navy boats in them and we get decent suits. One Saturday when the Port watch had liberty we wore our work uniforms ashore to meet Hyzer and go dancing. On the way to the club we were besieged by autograph hounds who, when we had our shore leaves on, paid no attention to us. However, with the faintest suggestion of uniforms we were the cock of the walk. The paddle-boating was indeed fun. When we came back we were soaked but gleaming with the sport of it.
    Another time six of us were passing a second hand Schapurinder- when a pile of old high hats caught our eye. In less than five minutes we were all be-hatted and one mark less. A high topper for 25¢. Some fun, eh!

a page from Peale's Sea Cloud *log, top*
Peale, right, and another Sea Cloud crewmate high-hatting it in formal wear
• *transcriptions begin on page 155* •

60

Sea Cloud

The year 1937 was exciting. There was to be the coronation of the new king of England, and Joseph E. Davies, United States Ambassador to the Soviet Union, had been invited to the historic event. Ambassador Davies was married to Marjorie Merriweather Post Close Hutton Davies, who owned the largest private sailing yacht in the world—the four-masted barque *Sea Cloud*. (Mrs. Post built Mar-a-Lago, an estate later owned by US President Donald Trump. HPH III)

Sea Cloud, a black-steel-hulled, white-teak-decked, mahogany-finished square rigger was built in Kiel, Germany, in 1931. Based in Jacksonville, Florida, she was being outfitted for the cruise to Europe.

After the coronation, she would sail on through the Baltic to Leningrad, later St. Petersburg, where the ambassador would use her for diplomatic entertainment.

public domain photo, Sea Cloud, 1948; photo © by R. L. Graham, Graham Marine Photo, Swampscott, Massachusetts

starboard bow of **Sea Cloud** *underway in full sail with a bone in her teeth, a prominent white bow wave resulting from high speed through the water*

Peale, 20, in 1937, the spring before shipping on Sea Cloud

My wildest dreams gained a breath of life when I heard about *Sea Cloud*'s plans. Two years before the mast? Wow! I'd settle for three *months*. Much correspondence followed along with trips from Hamilton, New York, the home of Colgate University, to Albany. (After Perkiomen, my father entered Colgate in 1935 and graduated in 1939. HPH III) I had to pass a lifeboat drill to prove myself an experienced seaman and furthermore arrange to be excused from year-end exams so I could be in Jacksonville to sign on before a certain date. All was arranged, and soon I boarded on an Eastern Steamship liner as a passenger bound from New York to Florida.

Arriving at *Sea Cloud*, I signed on as an O. S. for ordinary seaman, like any army private. Soon I got promoted to able-bodied seaman, known worldwide as an A. B. I got issued a formal uniform, including a Buster Brown skimmer hat, navy blue pullover, and trousers. *Sea Cloud* was stamped in gold on the black ribbon that festooned the flattop skimmer. Fatigue or work clothes completed our draw from supply, including a sailor's knife with its own steel fid, a spike used in splicing rope. Before leaving *Sea Cloud*, that knife would be used to splice, whip, reeve, open beer bottles, and open my hand. The scar on my left palm I still wear to this day.

First Day

The first day, the bo'sun checked out his brand new O. S. by telling him to climb the rigging of the towering mainmast. I leaned back, stared aloft at the forest of mast, topmast, yards white with furled sails and seemingly miles of hempen lines. Some of the lines, tarred standing rigging, shone black, but most, the more pliable running rigging, were light. Away up there seemingly lost in the low lying clouds, I saw the truck of porcelain cap that covered the tippy top of the giant mast.

The bo'sun was not going to be disappointed in his new sailor. I'd see to that. So up I went in the prescribed manner, one foot on each ratline on either side of the brace. I stayed outside of the lubber's hole where the topmast joins the mainmast at the first spreader, climbed on up the lower topmast to its spreader, swung onto the upper topmast, climbed to its step, and then saw that the last fifteen or twenty feet were straight up with rope rungs about eight inches wide. Up to then, my climb had not proved very difficult, thanks to my experience on the schooner *Cluett*.

Climbing wide, slanting ratlines compares with something like climbing a great extension ladder leaning against the familiar side

Sea Cloud, *port side, under full sail, late 1930s*
the largest private yacht in the world, owned by millionaire heiress
Marjorie Merriweather Post Close Hutton Davies

of a house. However, that last climb from the top of the upper topmast to the truck was a different matter. The tiny mast there did not measure much larger around than your arm with the tarred rope ladder completely vertical so that you had to lean back to climb. I finally made it, hung tight, and made my first mistake.

I looked down!

Far below on the little, narrow deck that looked like a canoe from up there, stood the bo'sun and a couple of other interested people, all with their heads thrown back staring aloft. I guess they fully expected me to freeze and wondered which unlucky fellow would climb aloft to pry me loose and get me back to the deck.

I determined that that would not happen!

Something I had not counted on did happen, however, and now you will be the only one to know.

On deck, a slow normal dockside roll becomes greatly exaggerated a couple of hundred feet in the air. I swayed in a good-sized arc, first out over the pier and then out over the water—or so it seemed at that great height. For the first time in my seagoing life, I got seasick! While tied up to the dock!

I could see me splattering the deck and being clapped in irons, keel-hauled, put on bread and water for the duration, and given fifteen lashes with a cat-o'-nine tails. I guess I turned green. I threw up but swallowed faster. I came down to the deck in record time, evidently passed the bo'sun's test, and rushed below where I finished the job in privacy.

Now only you know my secret. I got seasick while tied up to the wharf!

Soon we were on our way into the North Atlantic. I had earned my place as a real honest-to-God canvas sailor on a square rigger. I was also assigned to the port watch.

Due to a good skipper, some good mates, and a patient but tough bo'sun, we quickly learned the names and functions of the hundreds of lines, yards, and sails. We all took it very seriously,

Sea Cloud *mast crew standing on a footrope and unfurling a sail while underway*

since an error on deck could lead to a line loosened by mistake and a man aloft falling to his death, smashed to a pulp on deck or lost at sea over the side. Due to hard work on our part, the bo'sun's persistence and patience, and a lot of previous experience, we soon learned the difference between the port clew for the upper To'gallant, the main royal buntline, and both of them from the starboard foretops'l outhaul.

Mast Captain

I was quietly thrilled when I was selected to be a mast captain. Five men under me, as I recall. Mast captains take responsibility for smooth functioning of the four sail-setting teams. For instance, let's say the ship is sailing along with the wind off the starboard beam. The yards are canted so all sails are bellied and drawing full.

Say the captain wants to change course to the other tack due, perhaps, to a slow change in wind direction. The captain and mate on duty discuss the new course and necessary changes. The captain makes up his mind and announces the new compass heading. The quartermaster at the wheel acknowledges the new setting and prepares to turn the wheel as the crew prepares to set the sails. The mate goes out on the low bridge (low to allow for the sails overhead) and calls for the bo'sun and tells the "boats," which we sometimes called the bo'sun, what sails to reef, which yards to swing around, and whatever else to do for the smooth transition to the new course.

The bo'sun then shouts for his four mast captains and tells them in detail what to do on each mast. The jibs go with the foremast, so he might say, "Haldt, clew in the outer and inner jibs, pass the forestays'l boom to starboard, swing the fores'l and the lower tops'l, and have your men stand by."

Haldt then gets his crew, situated both on deck and aloft, to do the chores called for. In the meantime, the bo'sun has told the mainmast captain, the mizzen, and the jigger captains what to do.

As we became more proficient and learned to work together, the details got left out and the job got done quickly and orderly almost by instinct. A rousing "All Hands" meant, no matter what you were doing, all deck hands were to hop to it and get on deck at once. It usually meant a tack, in which case all men were needed to reset the yards and sails. The watch on duty could easily handle normal, minor sail changes.

Knots

The sailmaker taught us how to sew canvas using a curved, triangular sail needle and a leather pa'm or palm to push the needle through heavy canvas. We also learned how to flake a line, a method of coiling a free flowing line on deck so it could run aloft freely without any kinks. It looked very much like a series of Palmer Method cursive writing circles. We learned how to back splice and how to tie sailor knots such as the bowline and square. Sailors developed the ingenious devices many years ago because they needed strong knots that would hold under strain yet that they could untie easily even when wet and in the dark.

Slipknots slip, granny knots won't hold, simple overhand knots jam, and many other knots become impossible to untie when wet and swollen. A sailor can live with only the square knot, the clove hitch, and the bowline. Other fancy knots are mostly to impress shoreside friends.

Blue Ink

One afternoon after the daily wiping down of mahogany with a chamois and fresh water, bleaching the white teak deck (Clorox in the water bucket took care of that), and shining of the ship's brass, I was off duty.

Horror of all horrors! I dropped a half full bottle of blue ink on the deck. I watched in shattering fascination as the cap came off almost in slow motion and ink poured out onto the snow-white deck. I am sure I turned as white as the teak and was ready to die right there.

Our bucko mate was never known to beat a seaman to death, and on due reflection, no one ever saw him even lay a hand on anybody. He didn't have to. His tongue-lashing could rip the skin from your body in one inch strips like an Indian making smoked beef jerky. His withering look and the inevitable punishment detail that followed without a pause for breath sufficed to blanch the strongest man.

I looked at the splattered stain and knew I was dead. I would disappear without a trace and would never get back to Colgate to pass my makeup exams, or if not that, I would at least be marooned on a deserted island never to be heard from again.

Before the mate could see his ruined deck, I thought I would try to fix it myself. I rushed to the bo'sun, got a scraper, and was in the process of trying to repair the defiled area when I heard the mate's voice. He stood right behind me talking in a normal conversational tone. The jig was up, the brig for me to be returned to the states from our next port of call—provided I lived through the next ten minutes, that is. He looked at his terrified deck hand, at the half removed ink stain, and at the little pile of blue tinted scrapings.

"Go to the bo'sun, Haldt. Get some Clorox, and it will all bleach away." With that, he turned and casually strolled toward the bridge. I did, it did, and that rough, tough mate had a friend for life.

HMS Queen Mary

One beautiful, breezy afternoon, sunny and exhilarating, we ran with a following wind and green water curling over the lee rail. Suddenly an "all hands" brought us tumbling to the deck. A surprising course change. Turned out that the owner's daughter and her party were on the HMS *Queen Mary* out of New York speeding its way to Southampton, England. She would come up on our port stern, and we should look smart and in full sail as she passed by.

We truly must have looked beautiful. The *Queen Mary* changed her course slightly to pull within a mile or two of us. Ships' horns saluted each other as passengers lined the rails, waved, and took pictures. We were all proud, pleased, and thrilled. We learned later that we had been indeed a handsome sight—all sails full and pulling, bow rising and falling into each wave, and us leaving a wake like the best China tea clipper ever.

The ship's radio operator (Sparks was his inevitable nickname) told us of a change in plans. No coronation for us after all. We would go directly to Kiel, Germany, where *Sea Cloud* had been built. We would go up on the ways, have our bottom scraped and repainted, minor adjustments attended to, and then be on our way to the Baltic.

Kieler Kanoe Klub

At Kiel harbor, we anchored in the roadstead and waited for our turn at the dry dock. In the meantime, 1937 Germany buzzed with Nazi Brown Shirts and Hitler jugend (youth) groups. The Kieler Kanoe Klub (KKK) was one such group. Our full-dress uniforms and our being crew on a square rigger and a ship-of-state, we ranked way ahead of normal sailors. Normal in this case meant naval sailors such as those from the USS *Pennsylvania*, the German pocket battleship *Admiral Graf Spee*, some British cruisers, a Japanese warship, and a French gunboat. Those ships had been to England for the coronation and celebration and now gathered in Kiel for a little diversion. Still, we rated as the heroes —wooden ship, iron men, and all that. Besides, we were young, handsome, and well paid, a combination hard to beat.

German cruiser **Admiral Graf Spee** *in Kiel harbor, Germany*

In no time at all, I was invited to drink beer at the Kieler Kanoe Klub and shortly after that invited to join them on an overnight canoe/camping trip. I got clearance from the *Sea Cloud* and soon found myself on my way pulling bow paddle in a well-loaded, two-man kayak. About forty of such craft, stuffed with boys and girls, food and beer, threaded their way across the harbor, went around a bend, and ended up in a special campsite on some little island or other. Everyone set up tents, started a huge fire, opened kegs of beer, and passed out food with reckless abandon.

After dinner and half sloshed with beer, we formed a circle around the bonfire. The group held hands, sang beautiful songs, and swayed in time with the music. Finally it got on to bedtime, so they finished off with a boisterous rendition of the famous Nazi rouser "Horst Wessel." All club members stood at attention, threw stiff Nazi right arm salutes, and sang their hearts out. *NOT I*. I wore my *Sea Cloud* fatigues and was not about to give a Nazi salute. As the verses unwound, I first got wondering glances and then definitely dirty looks. My immediate neighbors began to whisper and mutter. With eighty to one odds, I decided I'd better do something and

Sea Cloud *in dry dock for repairs, Stettin, Germany*

do it soon. So I did. I stood erect and gave a good old-fashioned right-hand-to-right-eyebrow American-style salute. And then I purposely saluted the fire and not the Nazi flag.

My gesture seemed to satisfy most of the group. After all, I was their guest. And it satisfied me. The song finished without any American blood spilled. I have wondered since if perchance any of this group and I faced each other a few years later at such places as the Rhine Crossing, Battle of the Ruhr, taking of Frankfort and Hanover, and at the Elbe River meeting with the Soviets.

As the fire died down, my tentmate, who spoke better English than I did German, told me about a new and exciting Nazi custom. Hitler wanted lots of little German boys to be born out of wedlock so the state could bring them up and train them as full-scale Third Reich Aryan heroes, expert warriors with sole allegiance to the Reich. I don't know what he had in mind for little girl babies—maybe make more boys. My tentmate slipped out of his sleeping bag and disappeared in the dark. Soon, a warm, young girl came in, whispered something in German, and slid in with me. I said some nonsensical something in English that apparently did not ring of true love simply because nothing happened. There was no little Nazi in the making, but come to think of it, there was perhaps a slightly disappointed American sailor.

Schokoladen Kuss

While off duty in Kiel, two of us went to a nightclub where a little band played dance music. Our fancy full-dress uniforms acted like open sesames. Soon we were drinking beer and flirting with some cute frauleins at a nearby table. We up and asked them to dance. After much giggling and rapid-fire German whispering among themselves, one got up to dance with me. The oompah band knew only one American piece it seemed, which it played over and over."California, Here I Come" is a good tune for the first three or four times. They played it over and over in our honor until we got so tired of it we asked if they could try "Yankee Doodle Dandy."

"Nicht verstehen aber Ja, Ja mein Herr (We do not understand you, Mister)" and off they went with another version of "California, Here I Come."

Later on the reason for all of the giggles came out. It seems that, in spite of the KKK encampment, some girls remained puritanical. No one ever, it seemed, approached a young, lovely, rosy-cheeked German girl and flat out said, "Let's dance." Instead, there should have been sidelong glances, guarded smiles, introductions, clever repartee, a sly suggestion, a subtle hint or two, and then a politely worded request for a dance. They considered our brazen, typically American, head-on approach unique and delightfully naughty. They would consider it even more naughty for a girl to blushingly say "Ja voll" the first time around. On the way to her home, my education caused me to learn about "Schokoladen Kuss." One of you chews a chocolate sweet, but both of you enjoy its flavor!

Beerhall

The port watch went ashore one evening and took on beer with sailors from some of the warships. They traveled well along the road to getting sloshed. Because the Japanese and German languages are about as unrelated as a smallmouth bass is to buttered popcorn, the drinkers couldn't understand one another unless they used the one language they both had in common, English, which some of them spoke fluently. Without even trying, we couldn't help but overhear them. The Japanese made for poor drinkers, so most of them became loud, ill-mannered, and headed for trouble. That trouble came swiftly, unexpectedly, and efficiently.

One young Japanese sailor, formerly a student at one of the California colleges, it turned out, spoke near perfect English. He swayed to his feet from the wall bench where he sat, looked squarely at us, and started to run through his well-stocked vocabulary of American expletives as he told us what he thought of the USA in general and us in particular. He added that his ship had brought a Japanese ambassadorial committee who at that moment was conferring in Berlin with Adolf Hitler about dividing up the United States. He would have gone on, but his insults got to one of our boys with rapid-fire events.

Our shipmate got up and, before any of us could let out a yelp, lifted the Japanese sailor off his feet and slammed his head back against the wall so hard that the man lost consciousness before he slid back to the bench. It was deadly quiet for a moment or two. Then all hell broke loose. We formed a musk-ox-like circle of protection around our man while German and Japanese sailors threw punches at the outer rim like Indians circling a ring of covered wagons.

World War II had started in that little secluded beer hall. We got slowly taken apart, but some passing sailors from the *Pennsylvania* heard the ruckus and poured into the room. The tide of battle began to swing our way. Soon, some French and English sailors joined in along with reinforcements from the German battleship. We had a real John Wayne ding-dong going until some whistle-blowing, club-wielding Nazi Brown Shirts joined in. With that, everyone headed for the hills. Our gang judiciously began leaving by an open rear window when someone zonked me on the back of my head with what felt like a Louisville Slugger. In reality, it must have been nothing more than an empty beer bottle. I really don't remember much after that.

That, by the way, accounts for the second knot on the back of my head.

The next day, a very official-looking launch came by and bullhorned to the captain who, when asked if any of his men had been ashore the previous night, turned to his first mate and so inquired.

The mate replied, "Not that I know of," and our captain so informed the launch. We later heard that the men from the American battleship had been confined to quarters, the English ships had upped anchor and sailed away, several French seamen stayed ashore in a German jail, and the Japanese strutted around town like they owned it. To top it all off, our big ship broke the dry dock and had to sail off for Stettin where the big German navy repair facility could handle us. There we dry-docked long enough to have the work done that we needed.

Frigid

In the Baltic area, we stopped in Tallinn, the capital of Estonia, and in Riga, the capital of Latvia, just before the Soviet Union swallowed both of those delightful little countries. The *Sea Cloud* anchored in a sheltered cove for a sort of holiday. On a warm sunny day, my friend Lee Altman and I decided to swim from the side of the ship. Lee, a Florida boy, at that time of his life had never been north of Jacksonville.

I guess I had forgotten to tell him that the deep water of the open Baltic is no Gulf Stream. When he dived in and hit that icy water, he let out a scream that seemed to come out of every large bubble that broke the surface. Lee set some kind of a record swimming to the launch gangway. He jumped up the steps three at a time, ran across the deck, went below, and buried himself in his bunk in less time than it took me to tell you about it. I have swum in cold water such as Old Orchard Beach on the Maine coast, reported to be the coldest unfrozen water on the east coast. Even I had to admit that those Baltic waters are so cold that only seals, walruses, and auks could really call it tolerable.

Nedenia Hutton

The next day, we swung the ship's launches over the side and made fast to the boom. The owners' daughter and her party went ashore to a small island for a picnic and swim. The third mate as launch captain and I as side boy accompanied the guests' shore party. The rest of the crew went ashore in the crew launch and had their own party down the beach a ways. I took some home movies, had the opportunity to chat with the guests, and spent the rest of the afternoon floating around about one foot off the ground. In

launch from the Sea Cloud tied up to the boat boom

later life, that attractive young lady became a leading movie star. (The young lady was Nedenia Hutton, daughter of Marjorie Merryweather Post and her second husband, Edward Francis Hutton [yes, that E. F. Hutton], who took the stage name Dina Merrill. Born in December, 1923, she would have been fourteen when my dad accompanied her ashore with the third mate. For a time after my dad's *Sea Cloud* tour, he and Nedenia corresponded by letter. Her letters begin on page 165 with transcriptions beginning on page 169. I wish we had his letters. HPH III)

The King

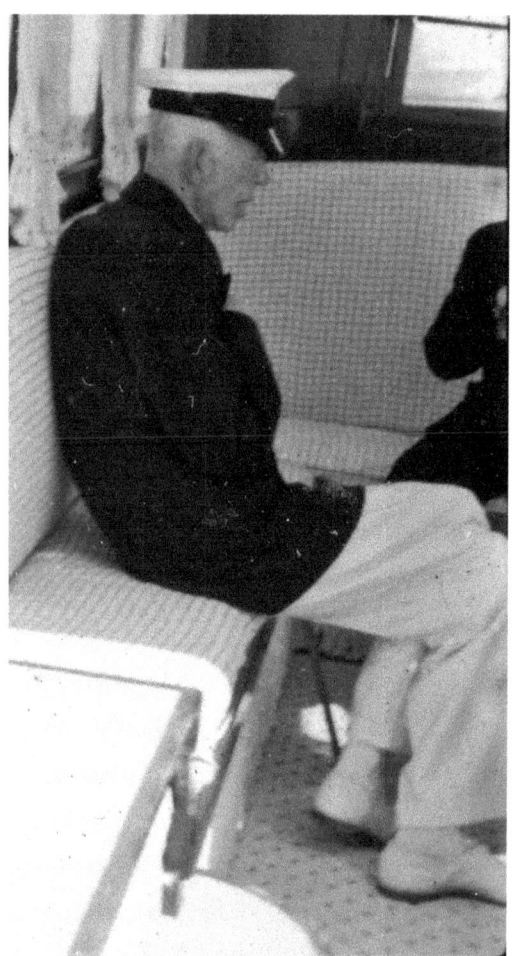

Gustaf V, Oscar Gustaf Adolf, King of Sweden since 1907, aboard Sea Cloud *launch on a visit to Ambassador and Mrs. Davies*

One afternoon, we anchored near King Gustav's summer home. He was the tall, elderly, tennis-playing king of Sweden and had been invited aboard the *Sea Cloud*. The passenger launch, with the third mate at the helm and me in my capacity as boat hook handler, went ashore to pick up the king and his party. They had just finished playing tennis, so they spent the time during the trip to the ship picking gravel out of the soles of their sneakers. He was plainly dressed in a blue jacket, white slacks, and white cap with visor—not what I expected a king to look like.

The king asked me about where I went to school. When I mentioned Colgate

Even the Russian who lives in the city can not leave unless he possesses a pass. Nice place, eh? In Moscow, I read, they are shooting men left and right for treason, spying and blowing the Trans-Siberian Railway sixty feet off the ground.... No Sir! Not for me... I'll do as the poets suggest and be a Scandinavian.

Thursday, July 15th –

Again a lot of water has splashed against our sides since the last time. Since then we have gone in more for social work than sight-seeing. Our first stop was Götenburg, Sweden but my job as launch-man made it impossible for me to go ashore. While waiting for the owners party I had a chance to leave the launch and see a little bit of the town but not all I wanted to. Later we went to the King's Summer home and he rode in in our launch. King Gus is really quite a lad. 70 some years old and still plays tennis.

beginning of Peale's log entry of July 15, 1937, about meeting King Gustav V while riding in he had his legs crossed and was picking pebbles from his shoe as no ordinary old man could do without breaking six or seven bones. His royal highness was accompanied by the Mr. & Mrs. Crown Prince. While on board he was sung to by none other than Lawrence Tibbet who is also guest on our ship. He and his wife came on in Gitenburg and are still here. Last nite he gave another "practice session" in which we were allowed to listen. All I can say was he was marvelous and even better than his reputation.

Again we moved. This time to Copenhagen the land of snuff — or rather where snuff got its name but funny, it's not made there. I got some one to stand my job in the launch and went ashore with the Bosun. A short evening but I saw enuf of Copenhagen to want to live there when I grow old. Quiet, clean, beautiful; all that one wanted. A toast to Denmark. But this is overshadowed by a return trip to Leningrad! Boo!!

more of Peale's log commentary about meeting King Gustav V

University, he remarked that he knew about that New York state college. He had a nephew or some other relative that had visited there some years earlier and had come back with glowing and well-deserved reports. He made several other complimentary remarks, and all I could do was pull a sort of Jim Thorpe-ism but instead of Thorpe's "Thanks, King," I was able to squeeze out an awed "Thank you, Sir." I never did get used to chatting with kings.

After taking the royal party ashore and returning to the vessel, I, still dressed in my formal navy blues and wearing that skimmer hat, started my usual ritual of washing down the launch with fresh water and a chamois. The procedure was to get rid of the salt water before it dried.

I happened to glance up, and there was the owners' daughter watching me work. I was still not over the thrill of talking to King Gustav and was certainly not used to being watched by that young lady. I don't know how it happened, but the next thing I knew, I was overboard with the bucket in one hand and the chamois in the other. When I surfaced I still had them. Somehow, I retrieved my hat and struggled back into the launch—thoroughly soaked and burning with mortification.

It was days before I got over that. The bo'sun congratulated me for not having lost the bucket.

Intourist

Leningrad was our home port, since it was the nearest deepwater harbor convenient for Ambassador Davies to get from his duties in Moscow to the ship. The crew had certain shore leave privileges that regular passenger liner people didn't have. We were a ship of state even in Russia, and we were a beautiful square rigger to boot. Nevertheless, when we did go ashore, we always had people tailing us. Had we broken a rule such as having a hidden camera, I am sure our watchdogs would accidentally just happen along to take it away from us.

The Intourist people arranged for well-supervised sightseeing tours for us crew members. Intourist is the highly trained group of Soviet public relations people whose sole job, it seemed, was to fill us as full of propaganda as possible so that we would go back to where we came from and spend the rest of our lives telling our friends and neighbors how wrong everything was where we lived and how right everything could be if we were all Communists. A great idea, perhaps, but it sure bombed out, as you will soon see.

One morning, two Intourist buses pulled up alongside us at the pier. When we boarded them, we saw every other seat occupied by a number of good-looking, well-dressed, and apparently well-educated girls. Each wore western-style clothes and makeup, the latter overdone to the point of being ridiculous. The girls all spoke passable English and were to be our guides for the day. It was their duty to spoon feed us large doses of propaganda along with a well-rehearsed sightseeing commentary. The plan was to drive to the Peterhof, formerly the czar's summer palace some few miles outside of Leningrad. It was a showplace used by the Communist regime to show how the poor working people had been ruthlessly used by the czar and all of his upper-class compatriots. In the Soviet Socialist Republic, of course, there was no exploitation of the poor. Everybody belonged to one big happy family where no one person owned anything and everybody shared in owning everything.

Bull!

One time, our buses stopped at a ground level rail crossing miles from town. The surrounding farmland was so flat one could see for miles in either direction. When we asked why the stop, we were told it was for safety's sake. A speeding express would be right along. We could see nothing forever in either direction, but we waited. Soon, off in the distance a steam train appeared, swished past, and we were once again on our way. The Intourist guides proudly pointed out how efficient the Communist system was."See? There was a train, and no one was hurt. Do you have such efficiency in the United States?"

After several bucketsful of such absurdities, it got to be funny. Their efforts, so obviously well-trained but so bizarre and

postcard of the Grand Cascade fountains at Peterhof, Saint Petersburg, Russia, built in the 1730s as part of the imperial estate of Peter the Great

ludicrous, produced nothing but laughs. They politely laughed along with us, but I am sure they were completely puzzled by our actions. At first, we tried to explain what life was really like in the states, but those highly trained and thoroughly blind girls thought we were either teasing them or were simply flat out lying. We gave up and enjoyed the ride.

Vodka

One evening, Lee and I were drinking in a bar, actually a tile-floored, heavily furnitured, ice-cream-parlor-appearing cafe where they served light meals, beer, and vodka. Up until then, we had never had true Russian vodka, so we decided to order some, having heard that the stuff was pretty powerful. We did so with some trepidation. The waiter brought each of us two thick tumblers, one full of room temperature water and the other full of room temperature vodka. He also served us a slice of lemon, a small dish of salt, and a large spoonful of caviar. By watching other patrons, we saw that one should squeeze the lemon onto the caviar, lick a pinch of salt from the back of the hand, and then chew a small spoonful of caviar. The vodka drinker then took a big swig from the vodka glass and washed it down with a swallow of water. We tried it according to plan. After the first swallow of vodka, we caused two sudden blurs as we slammed down the vodka glasses and raised the water glasses to put out the fire!

We soon learned the purpose of the caviar. When chewed, it released its oil which lined the throat and made it possible for the liquid lava to go down with a minimum of damage. By the time we had finished the drink, we decided that we were real experts. That, of course, was a serious mistake. By the time we had drunk the second glass, we found our shore leave unexpectedly concluded. A cab had to take us back to our ship where it took us the entire next day to recover. Our OGPU or NKVD shadows had the day off.

Of course, we saw quite a difference between that potent stuff we had in Leningrad and so-called American vodka. I have been told that Russian vodka was made from fermented potato peelings and was almost straight alcohol. It was cheap, strong, and usually drunk straight and true with but one goal in mind—get zonked as quickly as possible! Ever since that day at the cafe in Leningrad I have wondered how Soviet farmers live through their minus-sixty-degree winters. If they don't freeze to death, they stand a very good chance of dying from a massive dose of their murderous antifreeze.

Naval Cadet

Another time, we met up with a young Soviet naval cadet from the island of Kronstadt. In those days, Kronstadt was an important training center for the Soviet navy and headquarters for the Baltic fleet. The highly educated fellow spoke passable English. As we got to know each other better—we being from a square rigger and he being from the academy—we found we had a lot of common ground to work from. He finally asked if he could see our guns. We said we had none. He said he knew that all Americans carried guns to protect themselves from marauding Indians who stole into our cities to kidnap women and children and also to protect ourselves from criminals who broke into our homes to rob and steal.

We were aghast. Please keep in mind that this man was of the elite. He would compare in intelligence with a West Point, Annapolis, or Air Force cadet. When we assured him we had no guns, that we did not exploit the American Indian, that they did not have to raid our cities to stay alive, that armies of armed bandits did not sweep through our homes, he would not believe us. He knew what he said was true. He had been so taught ever since he was a kid. We were liars trying to protect our decadent homeland. Under Communism, there was no such thing as Indian raids, and no such things as armed robbers, the Underworld, or organized crime. In the states, we had Al Capone, Legs Diamond, Jimmy Cagney, and Little Caesar, didn't we? The Hollywood products he had been allowed to see were very carefully selected.

A little bit of truth with a whole lot of wild accusations made a weird picture. It was a few years before Hitler, Goebbels, Mussolini, Peron, Tito, Chou, and other dictators big and small made a science of the big lie. Repeat it often and loud, and it becomes the truth.

Our conversation deteriorated rapidly. As a matter of fact, it got downright ugly, so we decided to break it off and return to our ship. Leningrad was no place to start a fight. That we knew. Siberia was only a short train ride away!

Despite the ban on cameras, I managed to get some movies of the harbor by wrapping my eighteen-millimeter Kodak in a towel with only the lens peeking out of a fold. I innocently carried the towel-wrapped camera on deck under my arm and triggered it whenever I thought I saw something interesting within its range. I took some footage of a sleek-surfaced submarine, some soldiers on the dock guarding our ship (guarding us from them or them from us?), and a few frames of the dull, uninteresting skyline. A very unsuccessful bit of cinematography—but safe.

The Soviet customs people knew that American dollars were worth much more than the official four rubles to the dollar, the pegged price at that time. Our officers asked us to turn in our money; it would be locked in the ship's safe until we left the area of Soviet influence and then returned. We gave them some but also kept some. I peeled off a few bills and hid them in a brass cap bolt that was part of the emergency steering mechanism. When we went ashore, I removed a few, stuffed them inside my stocking, and wandered down the gangplank. Ashore we could get ten to fifteen rubles for each dollar bill. Seemed that even Russia had its capitalistic sharpies out to make a fast buck—and at those prices, we were willing to help.

Hands and Shoes

By that time, our crew had been carefully trained by Captain Lawson, his mates, and the bo'sun into a well-oiled team that could do our jobs quickly and efficiently with a minimum of shouting or other histrionics. We had calloused and strong hands. We could walk along the yardarms as if they were city sidewalks. We used the tarred foot ropes slung under the yards only when reefing or furling the huge sails. We had learned to slide down the stays instead of taking the longer and slower route of climbing down the ratlines. The skipper put a stop to it, however, when he learned how many rubber-soled, canvas sneakers burned out in the instep by friction as we slid down the lines. As I said, we had heavily calloused hands, so it was the canvas shoe and not the hands that burned.

It was our custom to rub fat and salt into our blistered hands. In the early days, it stung a bit but also made our palms as tough as elephant hide. The old-time, deepwater, canvas sailor must have really been a tough fellow. (See log entry on page 86. HPH III) Here we were on a modern ship with all kinds of mechanical assistance such as electric winches. I couldn't help but think what a rugged life it must have been when Charles Dana wrote his masterpiece, *Two Years Before the Mast*.

We also soon learned that there was much more truth than adage to the old time sailor's expression, "One hand for the ship and one hand for yourself." On more than one occasion when we ran full with a strong following wind and our bow blowing through one white capped sea after another, we would be aloft lying over the yard on our stomachs. We would jam our feet into the foot ropes with one hand clutched around anything solid. Sometimes the sail would be stiff full of wind, the clewlines and buntlines having spilled all the air they could. We then each punched a hand hold in the canvas and used both hands to pull in a couple more feet of sail. We tucked the sail under our stomachs to hold it while we did it all over again to haul in some more sail. We kept it up until the whole sail had furled, rolled into itself, and lashed to the yard. If we didn't do the job properly, the wind could sneak in and blow a bubble, and part of the sail would start to flap. That meant you were back aloft once more to lash it down properly.

11

I'm at last beginning to feel the part I'm trying to act — that of a canvas sailor. My blisters have slowly changed to callouses and I'm getting used to the four hour on-and-off plan. All that remains to to get used to the weather. The night look-outs on the forecastle head are killers. Spray comes up and you'd swear it freezes on you. That, of course, depends on the imagination powers.

Tuesday 24th.

At last, the brightly painted hook has gouged a hole for itself in Kiel harbor. But that's a little ahead of the story. Wednesday last, the Queen Mary slid past us taking all of fifteen minutes to come into and pass out of our sight. I wanted to take some movies but it was a little too far away. We were still rolling quite a bit yet she seemed to feel them but little.

The weather has been clearing up quite a bit tho and Sunday we had a fair breeze. Thru the channel it was of course quite foggy. "Patches of mist —," as the radio announcer

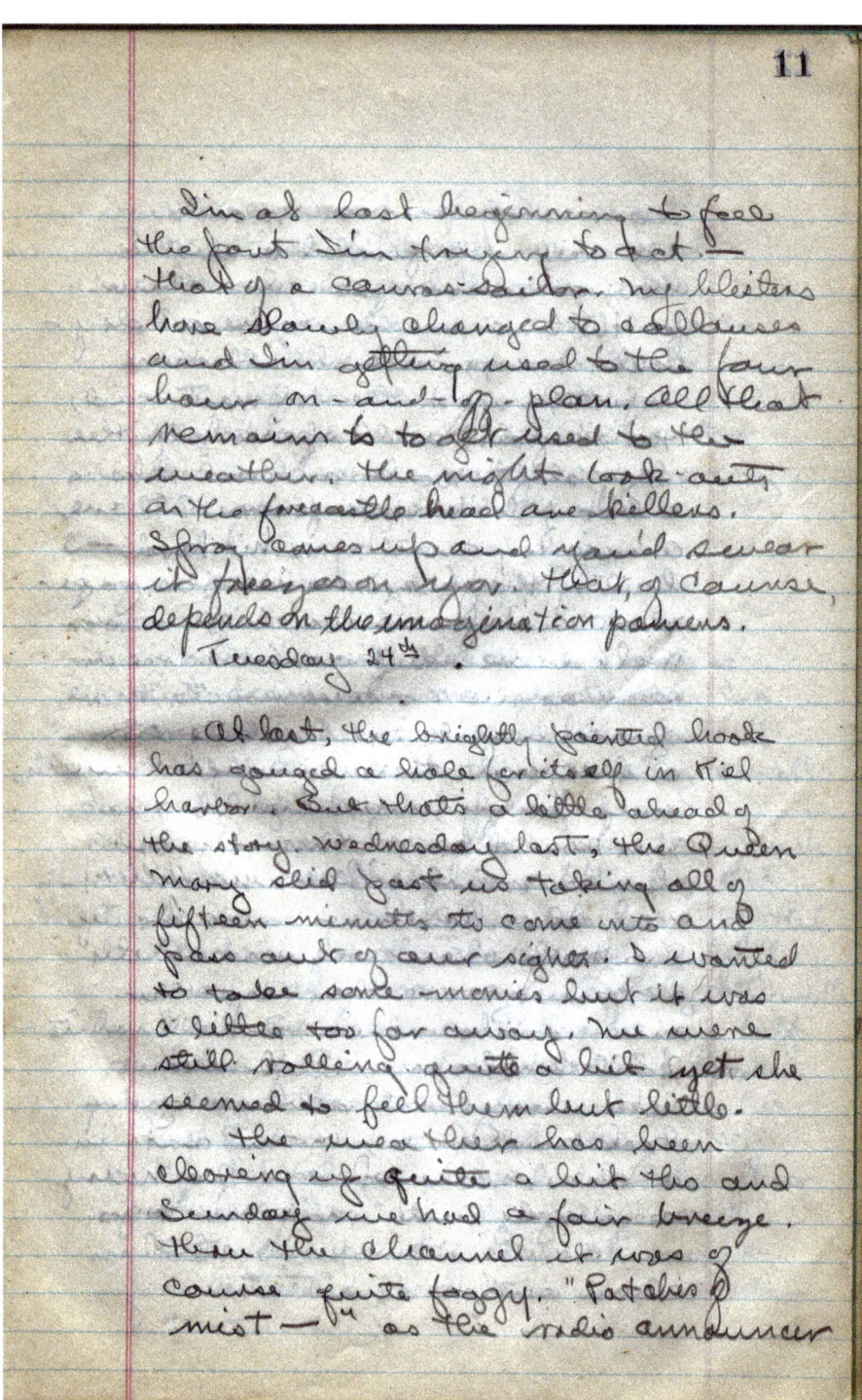

Peale's log entry describing that he "feels like a sailor"

We looped the lines on the yards and wrapped the last foot or so around itself like a new clothesline. We pulled the final loop tight over itself to hold the coil in place. Before I learned that simple trick, I coiled the line like a lasso and used the end to tie it to the yard. On one watch, the very thorough mate looked over every inch aloft through his powerful binoculars. When he saw those very unseamanlike loops of line, he shouted, "Who's the cowboy that just furled the port fore upper tops'l?" I had to admit it was me, so up I went to make the more seamanlike coil, much to the amusement of my shipmates and to my red-faced embarrassment.

Blind Date

The summer went by much too quickly. The *Sea Cloud* was scheduled to go down the west coast of France, past Gibraltar, and on into the Mediterranean Sea. I had one more year to go in college, so I paid off in late August when we once again tied up in Stockholm. A quick ride to Göteborg on a special electrified train, and I was down on the docks looking for a job on any ship sailing for the USA. I had no trouble finding one, but it wasn't to sail for another week.

I didn't have a passport, but I did have my proper American seaman's identification papers. The Swedish customs officer was not about to let me go until we had a meeting of the minds. He shrugged, stamped a passport visa on the first blank page we could find in my pass book, and there it is to this day. For all I know, I may be the only sailor with a visa stamped in my seaman's pass book.

Typical of a shoreside sailor, I had my pay burning a hole in my pocket, so I caught a train back to Stockholm. At dinner that evening at a rather posh restaurant, I had some trouble with the elaborate menu. I spoke no Swedish and the waiter, no English. I was trying to order more than the bread, beer, and milk that I had learned to say.

A young Swedish gentleman at a nearby table politely offered his services, which I gladly accepted. I had a wonderful dinner. We had an after-dinner drink together, and I learned that my new-found friend had a date that evening. He asked if I would like to join them at a public dance in the local amusement park.

A quick phone call produced a blind date for me. She worked for the Vacuum Oil Company, a US firm, so we started out as fast friends from the very first.

Our friendship lasted a few days while I waited for my ship to sail. She met me at the end of her working day, and we saw the sights together, dined, and spent the evening at a movie, or just wandered around. When it was time for me to return to Göteborg, my friends saw me off at the train station. As I was about to enter the car, a garland of red flowers was placed over my shoulders in the fashion of a Hawaiian lei. Some time later, I learned the meaning of the custom: a way for a girl to tell a fellow that, if he asked about marriage, she would say "Yes."

I left Sweden, it seems, in the proverbial nick of time.

Olle Olsson

The freighter I worked on headed for Portland, Maine. My days learning to work a chipping hammer came in handy. I worked my way from Göteborg to Portland without once punching a hole in the deck.

After I paid off in Portland, I decided to save the rail fare by hitchhiking down the East Coast. I was dressed in my seaman's clothes, including a black-billed, white yachting cap I had acquired somewhere in Sweden. That outfit, with my sea bag slung over my shoulder, attracted more than a little attention, so I didn't have to wait long between rides.

Having been with Swedish people for so long, I could imitate a fairly reasonable Scowegian accent. One person thought I was a Swedish boy on my way to New York to attend an American university. He was right on a number of scores, so I did nothing to dissuade him. I got a ride right into the city and had a free dinner.

All it cost me was the strain of remembering that, every time I opened my mouth, I had to sound like Olle Olsson.

Thus, regretfully, ended my summer on a square rigger.

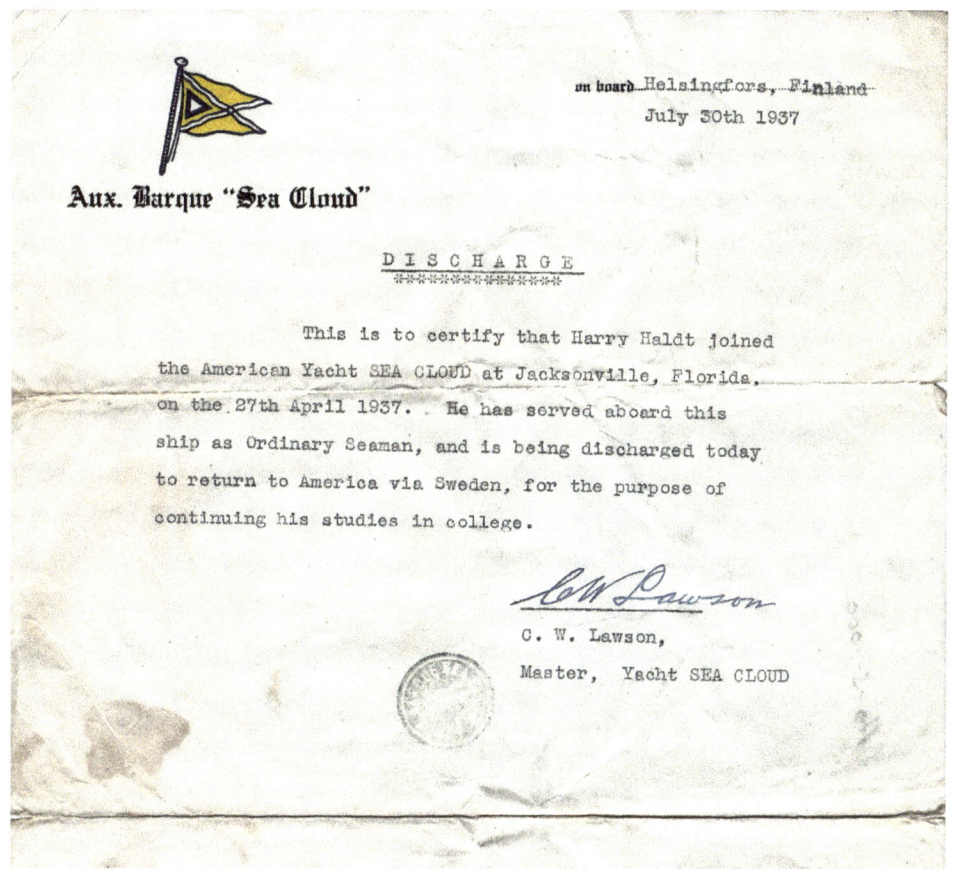

Peale's discharge from Sea Cloud

SS *President Harrison*
of Jersey City, New Jersey
built in Camden, New Jersey, in 1920
length 502 feet • beam 62 feet • draft 28 feet
speed 14 knots
July 14-November 1, 1939

```
F. P. WHITE,                                    ST JOHN'S COLLEGE,
TUTORIAL BURSAR.                                        CAMBRIDGE.
```

7 Feb. 1939

Dear ~~Sir~~, ~~Madam~~,

    Mr. *Guillebaud*....Tutor of the College, informs me that your son, ~~ward~~, Mr. *H. Peale Haedt, Jr.*..has been accepted for admission to the College.

    The fees payable on the admission of a student are as follows :

        College Admission Fee ..... £2 . 3 . 0d.
        Caution Money (returnable on conclusion of residence) £30 . 0 . 0d.
        University Matriculation Fee £5 . 0 . 0d.
                                          £37 . 3 . 0d.

£37.3.0

    This amount should be remitted to me at your early convenience by cheque drawn in favour of the Tutorial Bursar of St. John's College. On receipt of the amount your son's ~~ward's~~ admission will be completed and duly inscribed in the College Register.

                                Yours faithfully,

                                F. P. White

Harry Peale Haedt, Senr.

Peale's acceptance letter of February 1939 to St. John's College, University of Cambridge, England, for admission that fall college admission fee, £2 s3 pounds sterling or $9.34 US caution money (or backup funds), £30.00 or $130, and university matriculation fee, £5 or $21.75 when the average annual US salary equaled $1,850.00

These are the fares for a complete 'Round the World Cruise, commencing at Boston, New York, Havana, Los Angeles, San Francisco or Honolulu and returning to the same port. The cost of the shore program is not included and is $173.00 per person extra. U. S. and other port taxes, when applicable, are extra.

S.S. PRES. ADAMS - GARFIELD - HARRISON

Room Number	Room Alone	Each of Two Persons
7, 8, 16, 17, 21, 104, 105, 108, 109, 118, 121, 124, 127, 200, 201, 212, 214, 215, 216, 217, 218, 219	$1,455.00	$ 970.00
112, 115, 204, 205, 206, 207, 208, 209	1,505.00	1,003.00
*114, 116, 117, 119, 120, 122, 123, 125, 210, 211	1,642.00	1,077.00
*110, 111, 202, 203	1,792.00	1,159.00
†100, 101	1,792.00	1,159.00
†5, 6, 14, 15, 18, 19	1,786.00	1,159.00
*9, 10, 11, 12	1,872.00	1,208.00
†102, 103	1,884.00	1,208.00
†"E," "F"	1,917.00	1,208.00
*Suites "C," "D"	3,767.00	1,980.00

*Indicates private shower bath. †Indicates private tub bath.

S.S. PRESIDENT POLK

Room Number	Room Alone	Each of Two Persons
7, 8, 16, 17, 21, 100, 101, 106, 107, 108, 109, 110, 111, 112, 114, 115, 116, 117, 118, 119, 121, 200, 201, 210, 211, 212, 214, 215, 216, 217, 219	$1,455.00	$ 970.00
11, 12, 104, 105, 204, 205, 208, 209	1,505.00	1,003.00
*5, 6	1,668.00	1,077.00
*18, 19	1,786.00	1,159.00
†14, 15	1,786.00	1,159.00
*202, 203, 206, 207, 102, 103	1,792.00	1,159.00
†120, 122	1,792.00	1,159.00
†"E," "F"	1,917.00	1,208.00
†9, 10	1,872.00	1,208.00
*Suites A, B, C, D	3,767.00	1,980.00

*Indicates private shower bath. †Indicates private tub bath.

fare listing, above, from the "Around the World Cruising" brochure for cabins of
various size and
location on board
the President Harrison.
Fares for
"each of two persons, . . . shore programs and port taxes not included"
from $970.00 to $1,980.00, equivalent to from
$17,588.00 to $35,900.00 in 2019 dollars

cover of the
sailing schedule for
American President Lines
round world services,
December 30, 1938, left with
President Harrison
voyage No. 48,
Peale's trip leaving
New York on July 14, 1939, and arriving back in
New York on
November 1, 1939

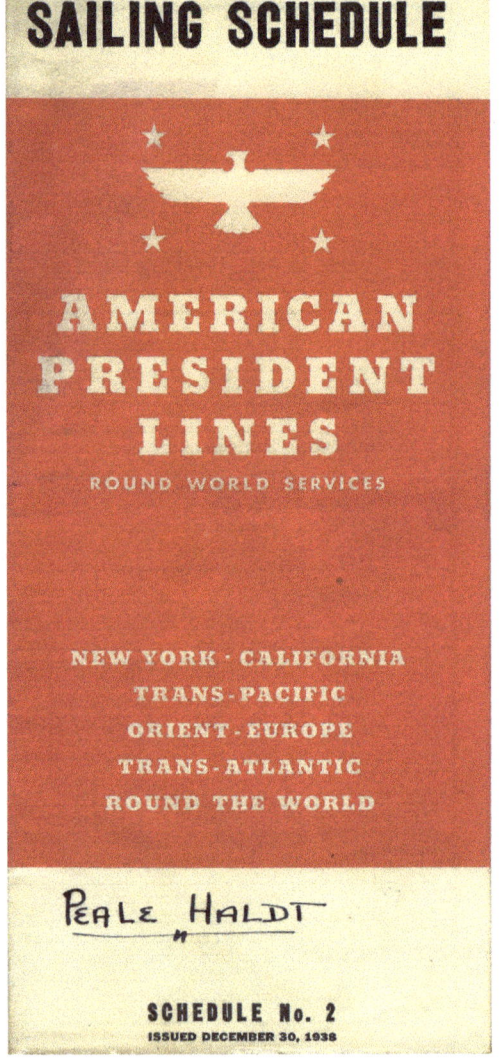

cover of the President Liner World Services brochure showing maps on the following two pages for
the world cruise route in red line for a total of 26,180 nautical miles, stops in bold print, and offices/agents around the world

GULF OF ALASKA
VICTORIA
SEATTLE
SAN FRANCISCO
LOS ANGELES
UNITED STATES
BOSTON
NEW YORK
ROUND THE WORLD
PACIFIC
OCEAN
HONOLULU
ISLANDS
MEXICO
GULF OF MEXICO
WEST INDIES
CARIBBEAN SEA
COLOMBIA
ECUADOR
BRAZIL
PERU
HUDSON BAY
Reproduced by permission of
Branch Hydrographic Office,
U.S. Navy
San Francisco, California.

Cristobal . . . to . Balboa
Balboa . . . . . to . Los Angeles . . . 2914
Los Angeles . . to . San Francisco . . 374
San Francisco . to . Honolulu 2091
Honolulu . . . to . Yokohama . . . 3394
Yokohama . . . to . Kobe 346
Kobe . . . . . . to . Shanghai 776
Shanghai . . . to . Hong Kong
Hong Kong . . to . Manila
Manila . . . . . to . Singapore
Bombay . . . . . to . Suez 2961
Suez . . . . to . Port Said 88
Port Said . . . to . Alexandria . . . 156
Alexandria . . . to . Naples 1007
Naples . . . . . to . Genoa
Genoa . . . . . . to . Marseilles . . . 197
Marseilles . . . to . New York . . . 3976
New York . . . . to . Boston 270
Boston . . . . . . to . New York . . . 270
Round-Trip, San Francisco to Manila 16102
Total Mileage Round the World 26180
*One Nautical Mile Equals 1⅙ Land Miles
CHINA
PERSIA
AFGHANISTAN
BALUCHISTAN
NEPAL
BHUTAN
INDIA
BOMBAY
Calcutta
Madras
BAY OF BENGAL
ARABIAN SEA
CEYLON
COLOMBO
BURMA
PENANG
SINGAPORE
BORNEO
SHANGHAI
HONG KONG
MANILA
ILOILO
CEBU
ZAMBOANGA
YELLOW SEA
CHINA SEA
JAVA SEA
INDIAN OCEAN
CASPIAN SEA
PERSIAN GULF

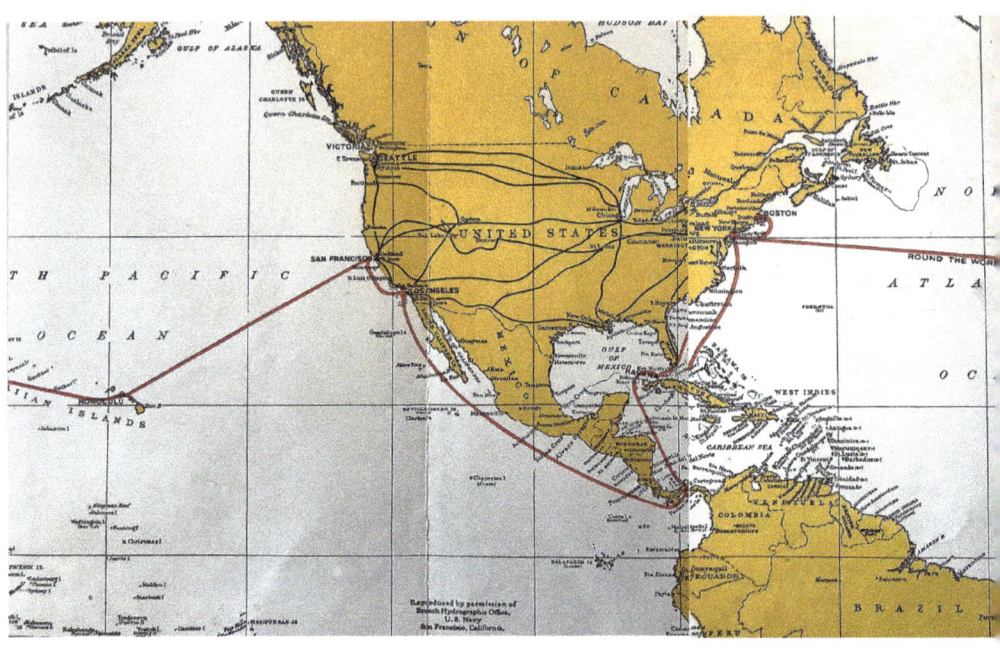

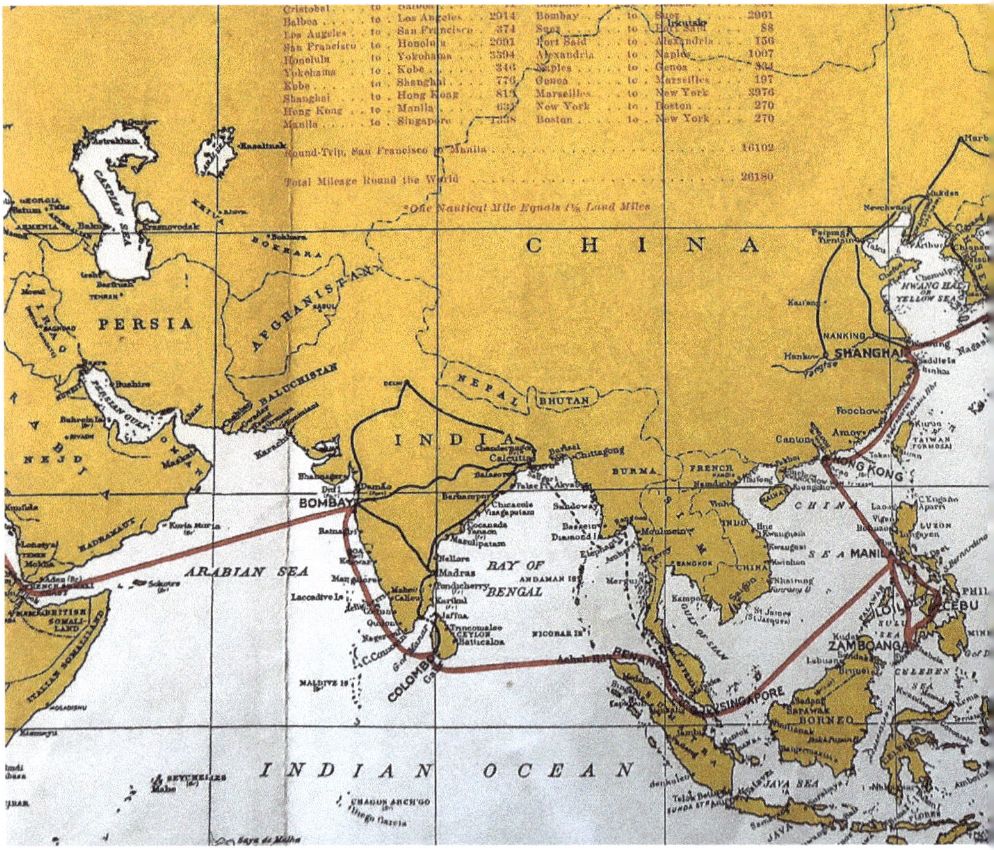

maps, left and below in slightly different scales, with round-the-world route in red line of 1939 President Harrison *cruise that Peale worked*

ITINERARY OF THE CRUISE

1st Day   **NEW YORK.** Sail at 6:00 p.m.
5th Day   **HAVANA.** Call.
9th Day   **PANAMA CANAL.** Pass through the Canal.
19th Day   **LOS ANGELES.** Sail.
23rd Day   **SAN FRANCISCO.** Sail.
30th Day   **HONOLULU.** Arrive at 7:00 a.m. Excursion by motor coach or automobile to the famous Pali, through the residential districts, Diamond Head, and along Waikiki Beach to the Royal Hawaiian Hotel for lunch. Transfers arranged from the hotel to the ship between 3:30 and 5:30 p.m. Sail at 6:00 p.m.
42nd Day   **YOKOHAMA.** Arrive at noon. After lunch on board, excursion by automobile to Kamakura. Late afternoon train to Tokyo. Night at Imperial Hotel.
43rd Day   **TOKYO.** Morning excursion by automobile to Kudan, Ueno Park, Ginza Shopping District, etc. Afternoon excursion by automobile visiting Shiba Park, Sengakuji, Noji Shrine, Meiji Shrine, Akasaka Palace and the Imperial Palace. Night train to Kyoto.
44th Day   **KYOTO.** (Headquarters: Kyoto Hotel). Half-day automobile drive about the city, visiting temples, shrines, parks, etc. After lunch, travel by train to **Nara.** Rikisha excursion, visiting Deer Park, Temple, Shrines and giant Daibutsu. Continue to **Kobe** for dinner at the Oriental Hotel. Rejoin President Liner in the evening.
45th Day   **KOBE.** Sail at 2:00 a.m.
49th Day   **HONG KONG.** Arrive at 6:00 p.m.
50th Day   **HONG KONG.** Automobile drive around the Island, passing Repulse Bay, Aberdeen, Happy Valley and many interesting villages. Also excursion with guide, by sedan-chair and funicular to the Peak, from the summit of which a magnificent view can be obtained in clear weather. Sail at noon.
52nd Day   **MANILA.** Arrive at noon.
53rd Day   **MANILA.** Automobile drive around the ancient walled city, the modern American city, the picturesque native quarters and beautiful suburbs. A visit is made to a tobacco factory. Lunch at the Manila Hotel. Sail at midnight.
58th Day   **SINGAPORE.** Arrive at 7:00 a.m. Automobile drive with guide about the city, visiting Raffles Museum, the Botanical Gardens, the Chinese section and other places of interest. Lunch at Raffles Hotel.
59th Day   **SINGAPORE.** Automobile drive, with guide, through cocoanut plantations and rubber estates to Johore, crossing the Causeway and visiting the grounds of the Sultan's Palace. Return to the ship for lunch.
60th Day   **SINGAPORE.** An extra day.
61st Day   **SINGAPORE.** Sail at noon.
62nd Day   **PENANG.** Arrive on tide. Half-day automobile drive, showing the typical beauty of this city and its environments, including the trip up the funicular for one of the finest views in the Malay Peninsula. Return to the ship for lunch.

itinerary for the 103-day Around the World cruise of the
President Harrison *from the*
1938 American President Line Around the World Cruises brochure,
above and next page, top

63rd Day   PENANG. Sail on tide.
67th Day   COLOMBO. Arrive at 7:00 a.m. Automobile drive of seventy-two miles to Kandy, through some of the finest scenery in Ceylon. Enroute visit the Botanical Gardens at Peradeniya. Lunch is provided at Kandy. On the way back, an opportunity occurs almost invariably to see elephants bathing in the rivers. Sail from Colombo at 8:00 p.m.
70th Day   BOMBAY. Arrive at noon. Automobile drive to the Hindu Burning Ghats, Malabar Hill, Hanging Gardens, Towers of Silence, residential and business quarters, Gateway of India, and back to the ship.
71st Day   BOMBAY. An extra day.
72nd Day   BOMBAY. Sail at 10:00 a.m.
81st Day   SUEZ. Arrive at 11:00 a.m. Transfer by automobile to CAIRO. Continental Savoy Hotel. In the afternoon drive by automobile, with guide, to Giza to view the Pyramids, Sphinx and Temple of the Sphinx.
82nd Day   CAIRO. Morning sightseeing by automobile, with guide, visiting the Egyptian and Coptic Museums, Nilometer and Mosque of Amr. Afternoon excursion to the Bazaars, Royal Library and Blue Mosque.
83rd Day   ALEXANDRIA, by morning express. Sail at noon.
86th Day   NAPLES. Arrive at 3:00 p.m. Afternoon excursion in the city, including the Museum and Monastery of San Martino, and Solfatara, and to the Amphitheatre of Pozzuoli. Sail at midnight.
88th Day   GENOA. Arrive at 7:00 a.m. Leave by motor coach at 9:30 a.m. for a beautiful sixty-five mile drive along the Italian Riviera to Rapallo via Santa Margherita, Portofino, etc. Lunch will be provided at Rapallo and return to Genoa by the same route.
89th Day   GENOA. Morning excursion in the city, visiting the principal points of interest, including the Royal Palace, Annunziata Church, the Municipio, Cathedral and principal streets. Sail at 2:00 p.m.
90th Day   MARSEILLES. Arrive at 7:00 a.m. Half-day drive within the city. Afternoon free. Sail at 7:00 p.m.
103rd Day   NEW YORK. Arrive in the morning.

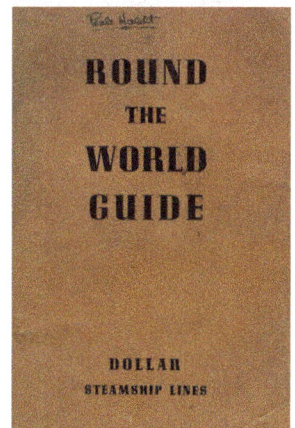 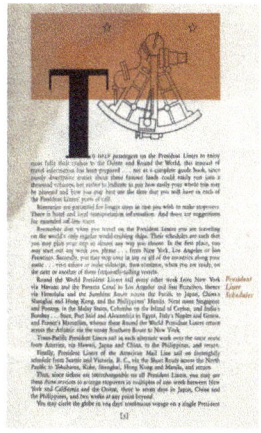

from Peale's copy of a stop-by-stop guide to the 1939 President Harrison *cruise*

*Peale's union cards, above and next page, for the
1939 President Harrison cruise*

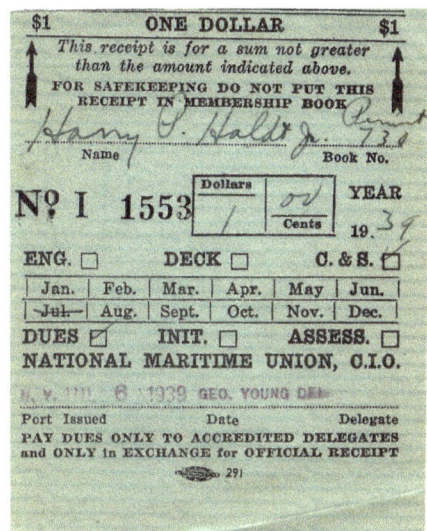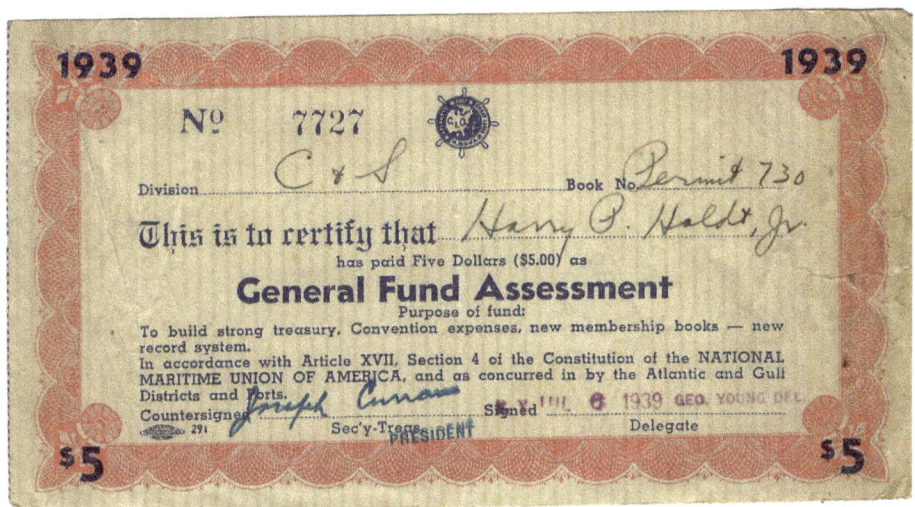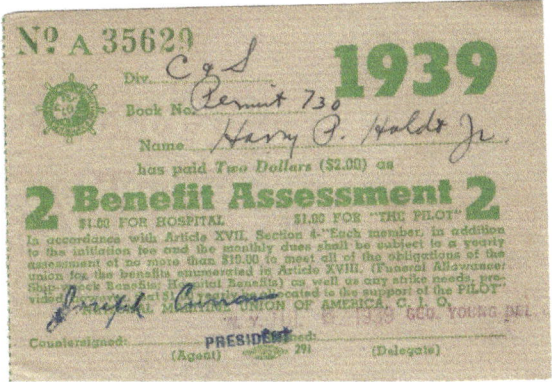

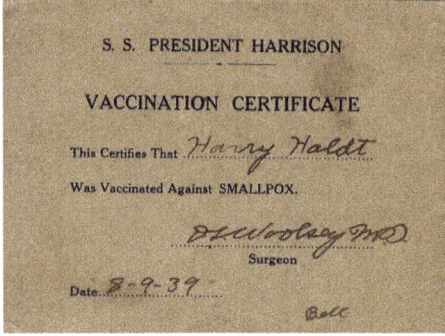
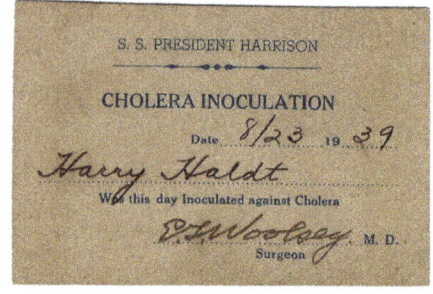

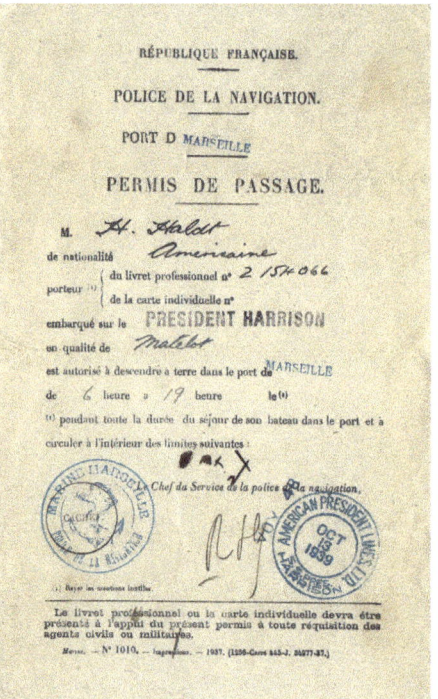

*Peale's shore documents for the
1939 President Harrison cruise*

underway in 1934, SS President Harrison *port side with an $ on the stack American President Lines, formerly Dollar Steamship Lines*

public domain photo,President Harrison, 1948; photo © by R. L. Graham, Graham Marine Photo, Swampscott, Massachusetts

SS *President Harrison*

1939. One last trip at sea.

I had made application to attend Cambridge University, been accepted, met my don or faculty adviser during my bike tour of England the year before, and was all set to start my graduate work in psychology in the fall. A plan began to formulate: try to get a job on a round-the-world liner, pay off in France, cross the Channel to England, and go on to Cambridge. I would leave the states in June and arrive in England in September. Little did I know, as I joined the National Maritime Union and went to the hiring hall, how world history would so drastically change my plans.

A job as bellhop in the stewards department on the *President Harrison* opened up, and I was soon on my way: Jersey City, through the Panama Canal to San Francisco, then on to romantic Hawaii and the teeming Orient—Yokohama, Manila, Singapore, Penang (in northern Malaysia), Colombo, Ceylon (later Sri Lanka), Bombay (later Mumbai)—then on to Port Said and Alexandria in Egypt, Genoa, and Marseilles. I would pay off there, go up through France, and be in England in time for school. A beautiful plan but one about to be changed drastically by my former acquaintances— the Nazi Brown Shirts and Kieler Kanoe Klub members.

In San Francisco, my trip almost ended very prematurely. The West Coast union representative spoke to me and said they wanted to put me off, but since I came from New York, they would have to pay for my passage back. They had checked with the New York union and had decided that the cost was too much. So I stayed on board.

Several of the "bells" paid off and left the ship. The bell captain's job opened, and I was pleased when selected to fill that vacancy. Then, we bellhops had a disastrous misfortune befall us. We had pooled our tips and planned to split the pot six ways when we arrived in port. Arriving in San Francisco, one of our cohorts checked out early and took the entire tip pool with him. We had had more than two hundred dollars in the pot, so we wished him every evil we could think of. He should get staggering, fall-down drunk, get rolled, and end up with a severe case of the crud!

Twenty-five-cent Shoe Shine

Bells at sea were a busy bunch fetching drinks, serving snacks, shining shoes, returning books to the ship's library, and so on ad infinitum. We had a little deal going on the side for a while. We designed little cards that the ship's print shop prepared for us. They said, in effect, that shoes left outside cabin doors in the evening would be shined for twenty-five cents and "Please Pay Bell Boy." It lasted a couple of weeks and produced a good income until some spoilsport mentioned it to the skipper. That little enterprise ended abruptly, and the extra shoe shine cards went over the side.

> There is a charge of
> **25c**
> for each pair of shoes shined
>
> Please Pay Bell Boy

Harrison *bellhops shoeshine card*

Each "little bell's" task produced a tip and, having learned our lesson the hard way, each of us kept our own tips. That was okay by me, since I had long ago learned that a little extra effort easily produced extra tips. You got out what you put in, so to speak. As bell captain, my duty meant seeing that the regular bells looked presentable at all times, knew their jobs, and knew how to perform them.

Doc

I learned the identities of the more interesting passengers. When someone pushed a button in a stateroom, a number dropped mechanically on the call board at the bell station. The bell captain would assign a bell to answer the call. All smart bell captains reserved certain calls for themselves, and I was no exception. Soon, a list of special calls got assigned to the bell captain.

Every afternoon, the ship's doctor had a cocktail party in his suite. When his call dropped, I was well on my way. Somehow, he managed to have collected most of the good looking women, which added to the pleasure of serving the drinks. He always ordered for the group, and when I delivered the drinks, there was always one drink too many. It took me only a little while to learn that he purposely ordered that one too many. A wink at me when I pointed out one extra drink to him, and from that time on, that one drink somehow disappeared between the bar and his cabin.

Being a bellhop had certain hidden advantages.

A handsome young mother and her equally attractive daughter occupied another cabin. The mother was in her middle thirties, and the daughter was in her high teens. In my low twenties, I fell sort of in the middle. I thought I cut a handsome figure with my ship's-barber crew cut, my brass-buttoned snow white jacket, my knife-edge navy blue trousers, and my spit-and-polished black shoes. The calls to that cabin always turned out very exciting.

But some days, time was as sticky as warm tallow. It was get up in the morning, answer calls, and read magazines for nine hours, eat, play ping-pong, and sleep. Another meal or two might be thrown in here and there as time allowed. When we had the evening watch from three in the afternoon to midnight, events altered thus: wake up, play ping-pong or sunbathe while exercising, eat, more deck sports, work with other bells, quit at midnight, and eat again. The cycle went on until we wondered why people do it.

Hawaii

In Honolulu, we took on a full load of passengers. Unlike on prior legs of the trip, we saw no band of man-hunting girls to get us in trouble. The entire passenger list of about eighty people was, with the exception of three or four tightly convoyed husbands, made up of the wives, sweethearts, and children of the US Navy in transport from Honolulu to Manila. The group included more than forty kids, and it had the makings of a lot of running around steaming canned baby food and milk bottles. It all had us wondering how we would make it all the way to Manila.

Blaisdell Hotel, Honolulu, Territory of Hawaii (T.H.) luggage sticker twenty years before Hawaii's 1959 US statehood

Surfboarding

Off the ship was another matter. One young lady wanted to find out about surfboarding. Two of us took her to the famous Waikiki Beach at Diamond Head. In our swimming shorts, we appeared just like anybody else. We didn't look or even act like bells. In fact, later on, while seated on the huge veranda of the Royal Hawaiian Hotel, it gave us a certain pleasure to snap our fingers and order cocktails from the liveried hotel waiters.

Another adventure comes to mind. In port, stewards and bells have little to do since the ship was practically deserted anyhow. Thus we had time to pursue the unusual. We went back to the beach the next day for more surfing. I had gotten to the point where I could ride a small wave standing up. Perhaps the snow skiing back home helped. Anyhow, as I got better (or thought I got better), I tried some larger waves. Those deep sea rollers start way out from shore, sweep in forever, and give good surfers a long, exhilarating ride. I sat astride my rented board—and please remember this was long before the advent of light, plastic, California-style boards universally used today. Those huge rented planks made from laminated wood were heavy, awkward, and cumbersome.

Along came a good rolling sea. I paddled off, got to my knees, and then, very shakily, to my feet. The sea got larger and started to curl. The surfers to my left and surfers to my right were well on their graceful way, their boards expertly sliding down the face of the big wave. Not so my board. In no time at all, I was tail over teacup watching as the huge, heavy, barn-door-sized plank twirled overhead about to come down and splatter me like a ripe watermelon.

I had presence of mind to duck under the water as the board slapped down where I had been. When I came up, I saw the board tumbling toward the shore that seemed, oh, so many miles away. I felt as though I was out in the middle of the Pacific Ocean—which, in a way, I was. The runaway board breached a couple of times, then slid off the back of a wave and saucily bobbed there waiting for me. By the time I caught up with it, I was completely exhausted. I climbed aboard and lay flat catching my breath and screwing up courage to ride it back to shore. I finally did so, kneeling all the way. At last I dragged myself up on the sand. My shipmate asked me why I didn't ride it standing up like everybody else. If I hadn't been so exhausted and waterlogged, I would have split the board over his head right then and there.

Dancing

After a few invigorating days at sea, the boredom was such that anybody who wore pants was in demand, even young bellhops. A dropped number on our call board could and often did lead to all sorts of adventures . . . like the evening dinner dance. During and after dinner, a small dance band played quiet, mood-setting music, but the few husbands on board could not and did not have permission to make a dent in the demand for dance partners. The few fellows and girls who signed on as recreation directors couldn't help much, either.

We were asked once in a while if we could attend these dances. A bellhop on an ocean liner, let me remind you, ranks two steps below a seagoing third cook. It evidently didn't matter to the lonely passengers, however. They asked the captain if the stewards department could help out with the manpower shortage. The answer was a surprising "OK."

We waited with bated breath—but in vain. Deck stewards and room stewards could attend the dances, said the strange communique. They did, and soon we heard tales of amorous conquests that defied belief. Bells, of course, the lowest form of life aboard, did not even factor into the unusual arrangement. We six had to wait for the drop of a call board number which, come to think of it, was better than restrained, respectable dancing.

In the early 1980s, business took me back to Honolulu. I could hardly recognize it. Still one of the world's beauty spots, but where there had once been oceans of pineapples, where palm-shaded streets wound up into mountains, and where little houses marched up hillsides, I found a forest of gleaming white hotels, neon lights, wide freeways, and wall-to-wall tourists. I understand that the outer islands remain like the Hawaii I knew when I cruised there.

Japan

On to Yokohama. In 1939, the Japanese were making their secret plans for world domination. I did not know it, of course, but I did know I saw more soldiers guarding the docks than ever when I visited Nazi Germany and the Stalinist, Soviet Leningrad in 1937. Riding the train from Yoko to Tokyo provided an experience all by itself. That suburban train comprised a combination of a Saturday night crowd on a New York subway and a World War I troop train.

Honey Moon Hotel

In the summer of 1939, two years before we went to war with Japan, an American visitor was not very popular. We sailors soon learned that we were about as welcome as carriers of the bubonic plague. Besides, our stopover was short, so we didn't really see very much of either Yokohama or Tokyo except for a unique sailors' haven with the appropriate name of Honey Moon Hotel. It was

Kobe, Aug 26th

Dearest Mom [Seeing how I'm in a small Japanese Sukiaki joint I thought I'd answer your letter that I got this morning. It was grand to hear from you and especially to hear again that I will see you Xmas time.. this A.M. we pulled into Kobe after a short stay in Yokrhama: While there cliff and I went up to Tokyo by train taking 40 minutes and costing 88 cents (Jap.) the guards wouldn't let us take our cameras ashore there so will have to depend on post cards. Here however, I used that fake press card and got the still camera ashore altho the K refused to let the movle camera go.

Peale's letter home from Kobe, Japan, written from right to left and from top to bottom in English language capital letters

a tile-roofed, paper-walled, tatami-matted, country-style hotel nestled on the hillside overlooking the crescent bay of Yokohama. It was a small, family-owned Japanese fairyland. The rotund owner, whom we learned at once to call Mamasan, was a remarkable woman. She was owner and mother to an amazing family, all girls, all young, and all very good looking.

They all happily served cold beer and danced to a jukebox filled with seemingly endless American-style records. They all seemed to have other capabilities as well. "Shawt tom" or "wrong tom," determined by the number of yen Mamasan collected, meant an experience unto itself. Any seaman familiar with Japanized English recognizes the games as short time and the more expensive but more desirable long time.

Bathhouse

In Kobe, we sallied forth to an out-of-the-way Japanese bathhouse. We hit it quite by chance while wandering aimlessly through narrow back streets not as wide as the fireman's sidewalk on Lathrop Avenue back home in Boonton, New Jersey. On either side houses of light bamboo and cloth or paper each had its cluster of discarded shoes and clackers. (The sailors apparently used the slang term clackers for traditional Japanese footwear, officially called geta. Geta refers to a kind of sandal with an elevated wooden base held on the foot with a fabric thong. The two supporting pieces of wood below the base make a distinct clacking sound when the wearer walks. HPH III)

Oriental Hotel Ltd. Kobe, Japan luggage sticker

Inside —and we were not in the mood to question the propriety of peeking—we saw men squatting down discussing, maybe, the price of wheat or what a dirty trick Mr. Hitler pulled with Mr. Stalin.

Anyhow, there they were—and there we were. Finally, we met a Japanese boy who, when asked in our peculiar brand of pidgin English, took us to the bathhouse.

Inside, we left our shoes in a box and passed through some curtains to a large tiled room with a sunken tub about eight feet across. One half was shallow and cool. The other was deep and warm. Undressing was unusual to the newly initiated as women made themselves quite at home every place except the bath proper. Their bath was in another room.

In the first pool, the cool one, one sits and relaxes while perspiration oozes out like sap out of a sugar maple. Then, standing on the floor, one soaps down with a good lather to be washed off by dipping little wooden buckets in and sluicing down. Then into the warm one where you remain until well done or at least partially parboiled. A bucket full of cold water from still another receptacle braces one up. Then on to an electric fan to dry off. When finished, one leaves feeling that even the cleanest clothes are dirty. Back on the street, we felt cool, clean, and quite rested.

Hong Kong

Then on to the British crown colony of Hong Kong with its bustling, crowded harbor full of exotic smells, sights and sounds—many times more so than usual, since the Japanese were at war with nearby China. The bombing of Canton (also known as Guangzhou, HPH III) 105 miles away sent streams of refugees into the British-owned and then-neutral cities of Hong Kong on Victoria Island and Kowloon on the mainland. While we were at sea, a Japanese plane had mistakenly sprayed the American President Lines ship ahead of us—I believe it was the *President Taft*—with machine gun fire as it headed into Shanghai, 760 miles from Hong Kong. Because Shanghai was under fire, the company wisely had us avoid that port and head directly for Hong Kong.

My memories of Hong Kong are a blur of strange sights, a seemingly endless parade of the mysterious and unusual, the whole seasoned by the exotic smell of sandalwood, incense, and spices. One afternoon, I rode in a coolie-drawn rickshaw up to the top of Victoria Peak, the mountaintop that overlooks the harbor. I hope

Gloucester Hotel, Hong Kong luggage sticker

that trip has been modernized by using motorized equipment. Never have I seen a man work so hard for so little. No horse could have pulled the rickshaw up the mountain as he did. I really felt so bad about it that I hired a cab for the return trip to the dock.

Horseshoe Barber

Across the crowded harbor was Kowloon City. There I had a haircut from a horseshoe barber, a sidewalk artist who hammers out one half a discarded iron horse shoe, files an edge on it, and then hones it until it is as sharp as any straightedge razor found in any barbershop back home. He trimmed my hair using that unique razor and a comb while I sat on an upended wooden box right there on the curb of a busy street.

A sixth sense seems to tell all natives who is a moneyed passenger and who is a poor, hardworking sailor. They also seem to know at a glance just what it is the sailor is after, usually the nearest bar and the handiest woman. Kowloon was no exception. The only difference was that many refugees had nothing to live on except what they could beg, steal, or con someone out of. A young boy whose name was as romantic as the part of town we saw—Ting ah Ling—tried to get us to enter a nearby shop to buy postcards and souvenirs. We couldn't get rid of him, so we had to grab the first rickshaw we saw and hightail it out of there.

One method of begging, and one so hard to believe that it didn't register when I first bumped into it, meant selling their children. Parents would sell you a little girl aged ten or twelve to be your lifelong servant. They would also sell the little child just for the night if you wished. It was truly a terrible and desperate sight. World War II was still in the future, and at that time of my life, the worst that I had ever seen were derelicts on the Bowery in lower New York City. On the cruise that took me to Hong Kong, I hadn't yet experienced the horrors of India and its untouchables, the lowest caste, which lived in and accepted lives of utter squalor that defied any stretch of my imagination.

Hundred-Year-Old Egg

In Kowloon, I had an experience I didn't appreciate for many years when a Chinese friend told me that I had been greatly honored without my having known it. While wandering around through the bazaar, I got talking to a well-educated, elderly Chinese gentleman who said he had gone to school somewhere in the United States that I have long since forgotten. We chatted as we walked along. He explained many strange things to me, and we found ourselves friends. He invited me to his home for dinner, and in my naive youthfulness, I accepted. Funny thing—when one gets older, one becomes suspicious of even the most innocent gesture. I was young enough not to have developed that deplorable trait, so we rode in a man-drawn rickshaw to some impressive small house on the edge of the city.

Small by American standards, the house was clean and neatly kept. The gentleman apparently lived in it all by himself. All I knew was that there seemed to be no other people there except an old woman who was either the housekeeper or his maid. (It never occurred to me that it might have been his wife!) We had several drinks the likes of which I did not recognize. Curious and I guess not very polite, I asked what each and everything was. One drink was a plum wine, the other I did not recognize at all and still don't know what it was. During our meal, the woman served us something that I had never seen before and have never seen since.

Two large eggs, duck eggs it turned out, were placed on my table. My host picked out one and offered me the other. Naturally, I waited to see what he would do so I could follow suit. As I look back on the experience, he obviously knew that was just what I would do. Equally obvious, I played it very cosmopolitan like it was just another day. When my host cracked the egg with the edge of his chopstick, removed one half of the shell, and exposed a tiny, as-yet-to-be-born duckling, I guess it must have gotten to me. I am sure I paled, then turned a sickly green and dropped my egg.

My host lifted the little embryo, dipped it in a special sauce, and ate it! Still the cosmopolite, I was not to be outdone. I cracked my egg, lifted the little devil out with my chopsticks, dipped it in the sauce, and ate it. Honestly, I don't remember what it tasted like, how I swallowed it, or why I didn't throw up.

My host, a lot more suave than I could ever be, then asked me very matter-of-factly, "Mr. Haldt, do you like oysters?"

Of course. Chincoteague oysters from the Eastern Shore are the best in the world.

"Do you like clams?"

Naturally. Cherrystones from Long Island Sound and quahogs from Buzzards Bay on Cape Cod can't be beat.

"And how about lobsters. Do you like them?"

A good Maine lobster is one of the best epicurean delights that God developed. However, it began to dawn on me that I was being led down the proverbial garden path. Sure enough, I had walked right into it.

"Did you ever think of where the best clam beds are? Or where the best oyster beds are? Or that lobster traps are baited with old fish heads, the more putrefied the better? All shell fish are scavengers. Clams and oysters live at the mouths of rivers where organic waste provides the food."

The rest I could already see coming.

"And lobsters are natural scavengers. These embryo ducklings, on the other hand, had never even been exposed to the air until you cracked open the shell. This is probably the cleanest food you have ever eaten."

All of his statements made brilliant, shining sense. However, nothing he said would convince me that the embryo made the kind of snack that would replace potato chips or pretzels and a scotch and soda or vodka martini.

I must have passed the test. After dinner and for reasons best understood by someone who had never eaten an embryo duckling, I wasn't very hungry. My host then offered dessert, some kind of syrupy, delicious fruit—and another egg!

That egg, however, was different. Encased in clay, it had been stored in a clay-filled earthen jar. When chipped out, washed off, and cracked open, a small kernel about the size of the end of your thumb tumbled out. One ate it as one would eat an almond. In fact, it did have a nut-like flavor that defied description. My host referred to it as a "one-hundred-year-old egg." To get that tidbit, someone takes a couple of dozen select duck eggs, puts them in an earthen jar, pours in a clay slurry, and adds more eggs and more clay slurry to fill the jar. The sealed container then remains in a dark cellar for "one hundred years," and the great grandchildren then serve them to honored guests.

As I said above, in my naive youth I bought every word of it, and to this day I believe I ate one-hundred-year-old eggs. Now that I am older and a lot less gullible, I begin to wonder if those things came from the local Chinese takeout and had a label reading "Made in Taiwan."

Tattoo

In Hong Kong, we saw shops, stalls, carts, and peddlers everywhere. You could buy anything—cheap. One shop sold everything ivory, another anything brass, another handmade shoes, another unknown smoked meats. There, I received the opportunity to smoke some opium. Evil-looking, skinny Chinese men offered to show us sailors all kinds of pleasures—tattoos, cheap drinks,

business card from Kwong On Ivory Factory, merchant for "all kinds ivory wares," Hong Kong

beautiful girls, gems at half price, white sharkskin suits, opium, and any other diversion we could think of. A sailor has the reputation of making a lot of money doing nothing, constantly looking for women, and drinking as much as he can in as short a time as possible. He is fair game for con men, pimps, and rollers from one end of the earth to the other. Smoking opium was out of my league, so I left that one alone right there.

The tattoo was another matter. A renowned artist in Hong Kong had a worldwide reputation built around a winding serpent of rainbow colors that twined around the forearm from wrist to elbow. For a few dollars more, it could twine around the arm all the way up to the shoulder. I was sorely tempted. I got all the way up to his storefront window, where I studied the intriguing display of masterpieces: "Mother," "Death to (fill in your own pet hate)," or "I love Maggie" or anybody else who came to mind. Each qualified as a true work of art. Whoever that unknown artist was, people recognized his work the world over.

Years later in Singac, New Jersey, a World war II vet opened a short order restaurant under the inverted tail of a heavy bomber where he had fought the war. He had some beautiful arm tattoos that caught my eye. I asked if he had ever been to a certain little side street parlor in Hong Kong. He admitted he had, and we were instant buddies. Sure enough, he had been to the same artist. His masterpiece, however, was not the multicolored dragon that wrapped itself around the arm. His masterpiece was a slightly smaller dragon that wrapped itself around a certain part of his anatomy that grew in stature as his love-making became more intense.

Incidentally and not to be overlooked, we still had a boatload of navy wives and sweethearts on their way to Manila. Hong Kong was just another port where some of the ladies looked for escorts to go out to dinner, take in the sights, dance, and have a few drinks and a few kisses. The stewards department upheld the reputation of the American President Line—"You ask, we do!" Even we lowly bells made ourselves available when the passenger picked up the dinner and drink tabs.

Manila

Prewar Manila was indeed a beautiful sight. One of the reasons that I especially enjoy my memories of those early travels is that I saw so many places that eventually were bombed beyond recognition and repair. Manila counted among those places. For instance, an old fort right in the middle of downtown had a nine-hole golf course laid out in the moat. I hope it lived through the war. Although the city had many modern buildings, it also had a great many bamboo and light wood structures that went up in flame, never to appear again.

Manila Hotel, Manila, Philippines, luggage sticker

Outside the city were uncountable little villages that looked exactly as National Geographic had portrayed them—one- and two-room sheds sitting atop bamboo poles, covered with palm thatch and crowded with squalling infants of all shades of brown. Under the sheds roamed pigs, chickens, and dogs, the garbage disposals of the time.

Coconuts

Some natives shinnied up the coconut palm gripping the trunk with their bare feet and, when aloft, twisted the ripe coconut until it broke free and dropped to the ground. It was well advised to keep a sharp look topside, or otherwise one might end up with a very sore head.

Those locals made a living by preparing coconut meat or copra. One showed us how they got the milk from the coconut. They peeled off the husk by slamming the coconut against an inverted, sharpened piece of bamboo embedded in the ground. Once they had removed the husk, deft chops with a razor-sharp machete lifted off the end to expose the enclosed fruit, and one could drink the cool, refreshing, colorless milk. I had to try the maneuver, of course. I could get the husk off after considerable trouble, but I never did get the hang of snipping off the end of the shell with two quick chops of the machete. Guess I was too interested in retaining my fingers.

Grasshoppers

In one village, and it doesn't make any difference which one because after a while they all looked the same to me, I saw some men squatting around a small fire. They gabbed away, laughing and seemingly having a ball. Curious, I wandered over and saw they were roasting little things on slivers of bamboo by twirling the bamboo over the fire. When whatever they roasted was done, they slid the blackened object off of that sliver of bamboo and popped it into their mouths as quickly as possible so they could impale a new one and do it all over again.

When I got to the fire, I saw they were roasting live grasshoppers or at least insects that looked like live grasshoppers. When they saw me watching, one of the men offered me one. In those days, one of my hobbies was to try, at least once, every strange food I could find. If, after that first try, I didn't like it, I'd never bother again, but in all fairness, I had to try it once just to see if it was any good. So I tried the blackened, roasted grasshopper. After all, by then it had cooked dead, couldn't fight back, and crunched.

This counted as one of those experiments that didn't turn out so well. I've not bothered to eat a grasshopper since.

Because of the International Dateline, Manila was a day ahead of home. (I learned to tell which day was which through the mnemonic "if it's Sunday in San Francisco, it's Monday in Manila." HPH III) Thus my birthday, September 4 back in Boonton, New Jersey, was really September 5 in Manila. But early morning September 4 in Manila was late at night September 3 in the states. Very confusing. That evening, I listened to a shortwave radio and heard a band playing from Frank Daley's Meadowbrook, a dance pavilion that used to be in Singac, New Jersey, just a few miles down the road from my home in Boonton. I have to leave it to your imagination what a thrill it gave me so far from home.

The famous Manila Bamboo Organ had made my must-see list. That someone created the cumbersome wheeze-box several hundred years ago alone is interesting, but the fact that bamboo constitutes all its pipes is almost unbelievable. To top it off, the crumbling walls of the church that houses it have withstood attacks by Chinese pirates, native raiders, typhoons, earthquakes, and, at one time, Spanish soldiers.

Coconut Plant

We had only a short stay in Manila, but I still had time to visit a coconut plant in San Pablo, about fifty odd miles south of Manila. When I visited the place, it was a humming operation where native laborers skillfully opened ripened coconuts, scooped out the meat, and packed it for shipment to the General Foods Franklin Baker plant in Hoboken, New Jersey. (Peale's father managed sales for the Franklin Baker Division. HPH III) I had dinner at the home of the plant manager, his wife, and two young children, an event that made my visit especially eventful.

During World War II, the Japanese easily invaded the Philippines, swarmed over the islands, and destroyed everything they could not use. The coconut plant became an early casualty. They took the manager prisoner and sent him to a male POW camp. They confined his wife to a completely separate camp and sent the children off to a third prison. They dynamited the plant and bulldozed it completely level.

The Japanese must have thought that the coconut milk was some sort of lethal chemical weapon.

Some years later I heard that the husband, wife, and children all lived through their separate horrible ordeals and after the war got together as a family once again. I have also heard that camp-originated illnesses led to an early demise of the husband and his wife. I wish their children well.

Singapore

Singapore in the Straits Settlements was our next port of call. (The Straits Settlements were a group of British territories in southeast Asia that in the 2000s form part of Malaysia and independent Singapore. HPH III)

In the meantime, you may have noticed something concerning when I celebrated my birthday. On September 1, 1939, Nazi troops poured across the Polish border, and by September 3, England had declared war against Hitler's Germany. I could see the handwriting staring me in the face. With what I had seen in Germany, Russia, and Japan, I felt certain that the United States would be at war up to its armpits. I could see my well-planned course of study in Cambridge, England, as a thing of the past. A telegram from Dad confirmed my suspicion: "Cambridge off . . ."

On our run from Manila to Singapore, I did a lot of thinking. I was part English and part German, I was on my way to an English college, and the USA would be in the war soon enough. I was a trained seaman, so QED (He means thus, proven. HPH III) Why not join the British Navy? Then when the states got in the war, I could transfer to the US Navy as a battle-experienced officer. By the time we pulled into Singapore, I had it all thought out and was ready to join His Majesty's Service. A few inquiries, and I knew where to go and who to see. The only question was how high up could I start.

Several cables arrived from home. One arrived from my mother, sister, and dad wishing me a happy birthday. The other from my dad, very businesslike, said, "Cambridge off. Interesting possibility with General Foods. Awaiting early return . . ." They all wanted me back soon, including the young lady eventually to end up as my wife. Very nice messages, nothing about the war, and a strong implication of come home now.

RCA Radiogram and envelope to Peale c/o President Harrison Stewards Department wishing a happy birthday from his mother, sister June, and Dad, received September 3, 1939, two days after the Nazi invasion of Poland

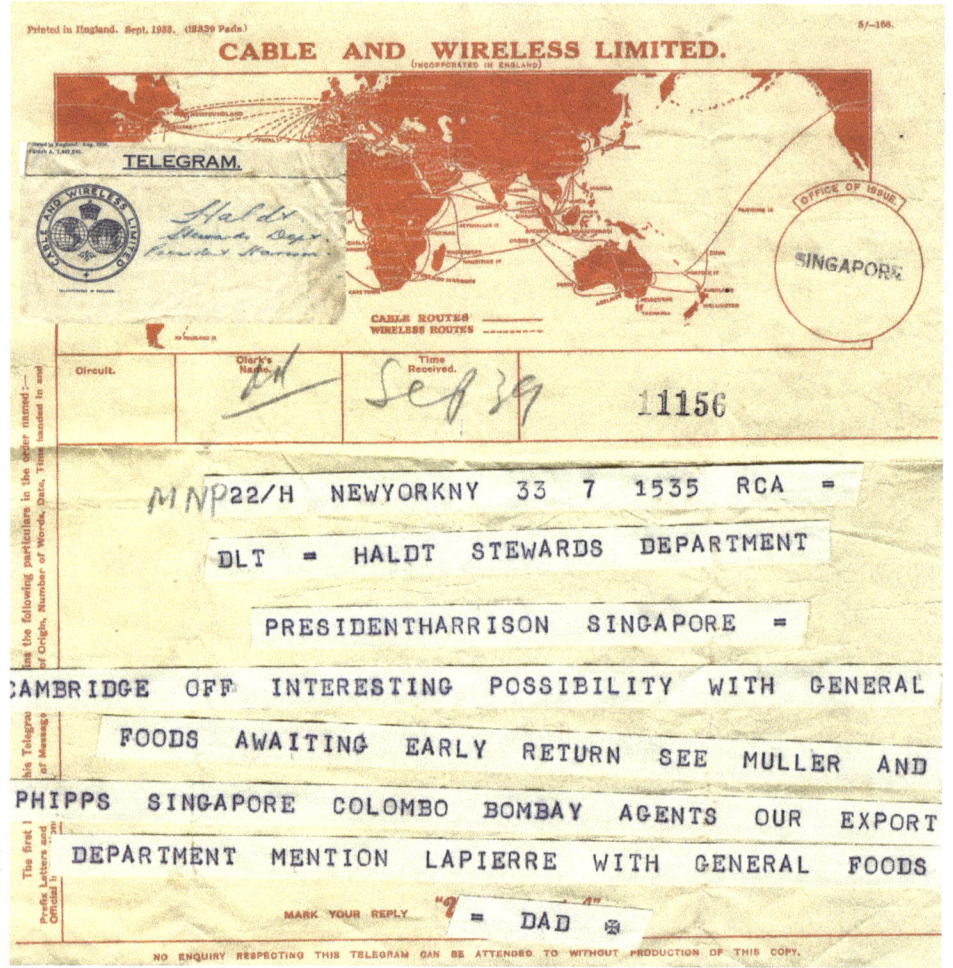

Cable and Wireless Limited telegram and envelope to Peale at the *President Harrison* Stewards Department from Dad. Great Britain had just declared war on Germany, making graduate study at Cambridge inadvisable.

Many years later, after World War II ended and I had done my stint in an American uniform as an army technical sergeant, my dad admitted to me that he knew perfectly well that I planned to join the British Navy. He also admitted that he knew me well enough to know that if he had said, "I know what you're thinking and don't do it," I would have rushed right down at double time and signed up.

And he was right. By not telling me what to do and by reminding me what a wonderful girl I had waiting, what a fine job opportunity I had before me, and so on, he knew I would think twice.

Which I did. And stayed on board.

I have learned to know my own son and daughter very well. I submit that this experience (and I know what you're thinking), along with many others, has helped me understand both of them much better.

Thank you, Dad.

Pre war Singapore, a fascinating island city at the end of the Malay Peninsula, truly earned its nickname, Gateway to the Orient. As in Hong Kong, I found crowded streets, alive with people, filled with strange smells and, it seemed, a solid mass of sellers selling and buyers resisting. We had a short, busy stop there, somewhat limiting my adventures ashore.

I could not, however, miss the Raffles Hotel. That awesome building and the town's principal square took the name of Sir Stamford Raffles, founder of the city. A Singapore Sling at the bar, where slowly revolving, large bladed fans and high ceilings kept one from melting, provided an extreme pleasure. No Singapore Sling since tasted quite as good as the authentic one served on the wide veranda of that picturesque hotel.

Raffles Hotel, Singapore, luggage sticker

How the Japanese ever took the island, I will never understand. I have since read that defenses all faced the wrong direction as protection against an invasion from the sea. I guess that's why the Japanese attacked the back door.

Well, maybe so, but the Singapore I saw was loaded with British Tommies, Sikhs, and Indian soldiers of every description. Warships jammed the harbor, warplanes flew overhead, and trucks blocked traffic all over town. It was the first place where we really recognized that a war had started all the way around the other side of the earth.

The more I saw and the more I thought about it, the more convinced I became that the United States would be in it sometime or other. Maybe I should reconsider the decision I had made to go home. No, hold on there. Go back home to a good job, get married, and wait until the war comes to you.

Penang

While I vacillated, the *Harrison* blew her whistle, and we were off for Penang. (Penang was a British crown colony in 1939 with the British Empire at its zenith. It became a Malaysian state. Along the route of the *President Harrison*, every stop from Hong Kong to Alexandria, Egypt, with the exception of Manila, occurred in a territory of the British Empire. The British had naval bases in Hong Kong, Singapore, Colombo, Bombay, and Alexandria. British soldiers controlled Egypt's Suez Canal. As the *President Harrison*, a ship from the neutral United States, made its way into and through the war zone in Europe, its neutral identity certainly came into play. HPH III)

We had a short visit in Penang. We were there to load on ingots of tin and be on our way as quickly as possible. I could manage only one afternoon ashore—enough, however, for me to see a sight that will remain with me for all the years to come.

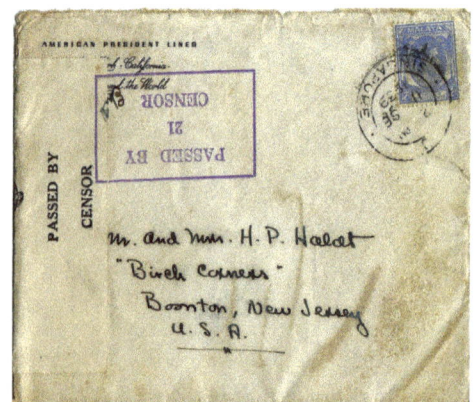 

envelope for letter of September 10, 1939, from Peale to his parents with appropriate wartime censor's stamps since Great Britain was at war with Germany

AMERICAN PRESIDENT LINES

New York . California . Orient . Round the World

on board

Singapore Sept 10th, '39

Dearest Mom and Dad —

This bright, hot morning we chugged our way thru all kinds of Islands and finally arrived at the docks in the Biggest Seaport on the Other Side of the World. Not until we were nearly tied up did I learn that we came in "the back door". It so happens that had we tried the main gate we would have been blown sky high. The British, not to be caught napping have laid a goodly set of mines out there. Now we are in here — none too anxious to leave.

But to get back to Manila. I believe I told you about that un-

Peale's letter of September 10, 1939, to home with mention of British mines

125

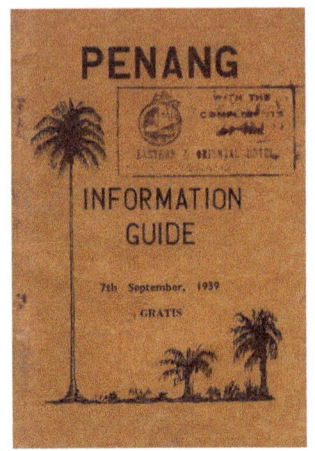 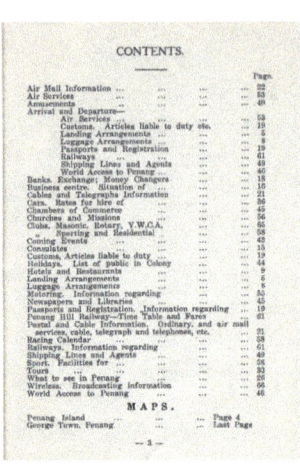

cover of seventy-page Penang Information Guide, 7th September 1939, compliments of the Eastern & Oriental Hotel, Penang, published every four weeks with map of George Town, Penang.

Snakes

Somewhere in the city, a beautiful tile and alabaster temple housed snakes allowed to roam at will. A member of the sect that worshiped there served as my guide. He had picked me up somewhere, for a fee I am sure. We entered the temple after removing our shoes and stepped over a raised coaming or water barrier such as found on a ship's watertight door. The raised coaming served to keep hundreds—yes hundreds—of snakes confined to the temple floor.

Those big fellows got bigger every year. They seemed to be fat and happy, and even though we walked among them in our bare feet, not one paid the slightest bit of attention to us. Maybe they were still digesting the last tourist, maybe they were defanged and didn't give a damn anymore, or maybe they were either just starting, just ending, or just in the middle of a siesta. Whatever, I don't remember much of what

Runnymede Hotel, Penang, luggage sticker

that temple looked like except that the whole floor seemed to be covered with hundreds of sections of chopped up garden hose.

The guide gained an extra tip when he told me that regular tourists did not gain admission to those hallowed halls. The only reason I was there was because I was lucky. He not only served as a good guide but also ranked as a member-in-good-standing with those snake worshipers.

He and his friends can keep them!

Colombo

Colombo, Ceylon was our next stop. (Ceylon, a former British crown colony, gained independence in 1948 and became Sri Lanka in 1972. HPH III) Places began to overlap a bit. We would just arrive in one exciting port when we cast off, steamed ahead, and tied up in another. Crowded streets, turbaned natives, Asian merchants; the smell of camphor wood, cinnamon, and spice; wood carvers, metalsmiths, tea merchants, cocoa vendors, and fruit peddlers— all appeared much the same wherever we went.

Forty years later, each morning as I get dressed, right in front of me sit two hammered brass containers. Some artisan in Kandy, an island city on Ceylon, skillfully hammered silver and copper onto and into the brass and finely tooled a

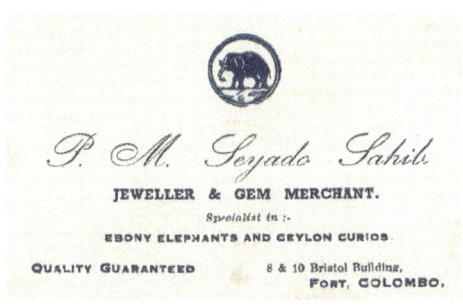

business card for P. M. Seyado Sahib, merchant specializing in ebony elephants and Ceylon curios, Fort Colombo, Ceylon

design over the whole thing. A Ceylonese elephant occupies each of the lids. We watched some of the workmen operate. They sit on the ground, hold the object with their feet, and work with both hands free to hold a hammer and engraving tool.

Zoo

Not far from the docks was a zoo the likes of which I had never seen before. Open as anything could be unless in the middle of someone's front lawn, it included elephants that roamed seemingly at will. Tigers in cramped quarters had long since given up any thought of getting out. Peacocks paraded around spacious lawns.

One cage in particular contained a great boa, a huge fellow. When I started to take a picture, one of the keepers rushed over, told me to wait, and then opened the gate to the outer cage. I was about to take off for the hills when he told me, "No worry, no worry. He just ate pig. Too lazy to move." With that, he kicked the huge coil and it slowly unwound to become the largest snake I had ever seen. Sure enough, interested only in getting away from the kicker with the least amount of effort, it bulged in the middle. I stood there transfixed, wondering whether the bulge was really a pig or a dimwitted former keeper.

At the same zoo, just like the big game hunters, I rode an elephant. With a little imagination, I could hear my beaters clanging their cymbals, striking the earth with long poles, and shouting threats to a slinking, man-eating tiger hidden in the tall, dry grass. My ever-faithful gun bearer was ready to hand me my high-powered rifle so I could bring down a record specimen with one clean, expert shot. Suddenly I got shaken out of my dream when the elephant returned to the loading/unloading platform and the crew unceremoniously ushered me out of my seat so the next paying guest could take my place.

Ceylon, the Pearl of the Indian Ocean, had lived up to its reputation.

Bombay

From Colombo, we steamed around the southern tip of India, past Cape Comorin, on into the Arabian Sea, and up the west coast to Bombay, known for centuries as the Gateway to India. (Name officially changed to Mumbai in 1995, HPH III) Prewar Bombay was a sight to stretch the imagination. If someone asked which city I found the most unusual, most fascinating, and most awesome, I would say Bombay without a moment's hesitation.

Taj Mahal Hotel

Early on, one of my shipmates, Cliff Beckwith, and I decided to go to a posh hotel and blow ourselves to an expensive bash, said bash to consist of a wickedly expensive drink served by turbaned waiters in an exclusive hotel. We settled on the Taj Mahal Hotel. We were seated in large, overstuffed chairs on a carpeted, open-air veranda, and sure enough, turbaned waiters took our order. We studied the wine list, reading the right hand column only, selected the most costly drink, and sat back to enjoy our festivities.

Taj Mahal Hotel, Bombay (later Mumbai) India, luggage sticker

Soon a group of waiters arrived—the wine steward with his necklaced key, a boy with a silvered wine stand, another with a large insulated server filled with crushed ice, and still another with a silver tray and two long-stemmed wine glasses. Man! For two bellhops, this was really living! The steward bowed, dug around in the box of ice, and with a great flourish, pulled out two cans of Oregon apple juice!

On a hot day in India, half way around the world, on the plush veranda of an expensive hotel, maybe a can of American apple juice was a very exclusive drink. We hid our laughter, watched the great drama unfold as the team graciously served our drinks, leaned back, and enjoyed it. We ended up ordering a run-of-the-mill bottle of less expensive champagne to wash the taste out of our mouths.

Betel Nuts

Chewing betel nuts, we heard, was the poor man's jag. It didn't cost much—less than drinking beer. We decided to try some—

you know, "When in Rome . . ." The particular main street had numerous large buildings with arch-shaped windows sunk in thick walls that helped keep the inside of buildings cool. The deep arches also served as little shops for all sorts of street vendors. One dark-skinned, white-turbaned fellow, who looked remarkably like one of Ali Baba's thieves, sat cross-legged in one window recess completely surrounded by brass pots and glass jars full of strange-looking things. We learned that he sold betel nuts, so we decided to let him show us how to get started with that oriental habit. He asked (in Oxfordian English, by the way) if we had ever chewed betel before. We had to admit our virginity. So he said he would make a small one for us to try. If we didn't like it, we could always spit it out. That sounded fair enough, so we watched him while he put it all together.

First, he took a large green leaf a bit bigger than an open hand, dipped into one of the pots and spread a thick, brown paste on the leaf. Then he reached into another pot and sprinkled some white powder on the paste. He then squeezed some lime on top of the paste. Finally, from still another pot, he scattered some little pieces of something that looked like broken peanuts on top of that. He then folded the leaf four sides to the middle so we each had a packet about three inches long, two inches wide, and an inch and a half thick. He handed it to us. A few coins changed hands, and that was that—except we didn't know what to do with the cumbersome wad. Did we bite off a chaw like chewing tobacco? Did we chew into it like a ham and cheese sandwich? Or what?

The gentleman saw our consternation and told us to pull out our cheek, slide the whole packet into the cheek space outside the teeth, and hold it there like a squirrel with a mouth puffed full of acorns. He added, "Don't chew it. Just let the saliva work into it. Once in a while, squeeze your cheek tight and spit out the juices. They will start to turn pink and then red. When the juice is blood red, it is working. But remember, Don't swallow!"

We should have taken notice to that little warning "when it's blood red, it's working," but we didn't. We did, however, start to notice other betel nut chewers. We saw the blood red lips and the black, and I do mean black, teeth of addicted chewers. We also noticed splats of red saliva that seemed to cover the sidewalks and streets everywhere we looked. We also noticed that bright, alert, intelligent-looking people did not have telltale bulges, red lips, or black teeth like only low-paid stevedores, rickshaw pullers, street vendors, cattle herders, and truck loaders who were our companions. We further saw that chewers rode in window seats of buses, many of them double-decked and open-topped variety, so we had to be alert for misdirected dollops from aloft.

We followed instructions and squeezed and analyzed our spit. Still colorless. We rode in a bus upper deck and spat over the side just as if we knew what we were doing. Finally, I leaned on my hand— and was shocked to find that my left jaw was numb. I asked Cliff about his. The same. We decided to get off and study that new, odd development.

At street level, we found that one whole side of each of our faces felt numb, and we had started to slobber red. Slobber, because our lips did not work properly. About then, we got sort of dizzy, too, so we decided maybe that damned betel nut had something to do with it. We spat it out on the curb of the busy street while we tried to figure out what to do to avoid, if possible, what we fully knew was to be a swift and sudden death.

While we moaned, a tall, spit-and-polish Sikh cop came over. He figured us a couple of drunk American seamen cluttering up his beat, and he was going to get us out of there as quickly as possible. When we explained what we had been doing, he chuckled and told us what we had *really* been doing. The uninitiated should not indulge in betel nut, it turned out. The leaf, he said, was a cocoa leaf, the brown paste was bitter raw chocolate, the white powder was lime, the lime juice was lime juice, of course, and the chopped-up peanuts were betel nut. The chemistry, as he explained it, caused the lime powder to work on the cocoa, and the resulting juice became cocaine. No wonder we got so sick.

The cop hailed a cab and directed the driver to the *President Harrison*. We returned from that adventure two very sick and unhappy puppies. Thus concluded our first and last experience in the dope scene!

Those Sikh cops had another job besides keeping American sailors from killing themselves. Early every morning, they walked the streets in the dock area where homeless dock workers, stevedores, and line handlers made the shed-covered sidewalks their living quarters. The cops kicked each sleeping body. If it moved, they passed on. If it didn't, they dragged the corpse to the curb where a following police van loaded the thin, scrawny cadaver onto the back of a truck for burial in some lonely, city-owned potter's field.

Cribs

Life in India in the late 1930s could indeed be pitiful. Cliff and I met up with a hard-drinking English tea plantation overseer in Bombay for a vacation. As we drank together and swapped tales, he soon learned it was our first visit to Bombay. He said he would show us around in return for an occasional free drink. Since the price was right, we soon had ourselves a guide. We saw famous temples, buildings, parks, and all sorts of landmarks, but nothing impressed us as did a certain stinking, dirty, teeming street down in the squalid red light district.

As we walked with the throng of turbaned natives, Panama-hatted tourists, and pith-helmeted white natives, we noticed dirty, unpainted storefronts with wooden bars instead of glass windows. Those cages or cribs were furnished like threadbare bedrooms—each with a thin, worn dirty carpet, a couple of chairs, and a curtained alcove in the rear. In the cribs, women sold their jaded charms for prices that defied belief. A pie amounted to one tenth of a rupee, and in those days, one received a palm of rupees for a dollar. The women charged from several rupees for the younger, more handsome, and less shopworn to a few pie for the dirty, haggard, disease-ridden old-timers. The street smells matched the surroundings.

The women locked the wooden cages on the inside. After haggling a price right there on the sidewalk, a customer agreed to and paid for her services. Then an animated pile of dirty clothes unlocked the cage door and relocked it after her customer entered the crib. A bed behind the curtain then got put to use for a predetermined period of time. Pitiful—and unbelievable. If one could get past the filth, the stench, and the repulsiveness, I am sure he would leave that back street of Bombay with advanced cases of every known pestilence plus a few more horrible diseases not yet identified.

Business card of Melwani & Co., emporium of Indian Arts & Crafts, Bombay "All Prices marked in plain English Figures"

Untouchables

In Bombay, a city of immeasurable extremes between the very rich and poverty stricken homeless, I saw my first lowest-caste untouchable. On a suburban hilltop, a sewer-cleaning crew lifted manhole covers and cleaned the city sewer pipes in a most unique and unnerving way. A dark, skinny old man wore a cap made from what looked like a woman's cut-off cotton stocking. He had a hempen rope about an inch in diameter tied around his waist that served two purposes: one, to hold up the ends of a tiny loincloth and two, to act as a harness tied to a line of between twenty-five and thirty feet long.

And that was all he wore.

His job entailed climbing down into the manhole and crawling into and through the filth-choked sewer pipe until he came to the next manhole, where he would climb up for air. Attached to the other end of the long line, he had a large ball of brush and twigs, something like the clumped end of a witch's broom. As he crawled on his hands and knees through the sewer pipe, he dragged the ball of branches to scrape and clean the inside of the pipe. I heard that once in a while, the brush would build up a wall of water and sludge that engulfed the puller before he could reach the next open manhole. When that happened, a reserve Gunga Din went into the pipe and pulled out the drowned body.

The conditions he worked under made him an untouchable. Those poor, miserable, casteless people in a society highly stratified by caste, counted as the lowest creatures on earth who had to step off the sidewalk into the gutter whenever a member of a higher caste approached. Some higher-class wore marks in the middle of their forehead to signify their castes. For the untouchable, a caste mark was completely unnecessary, since his personal stench made it impossible to get close enough even to see a mark on his forehead.

Everything I've written about here took place in the late 1930s. Let's hope that Roto-Rooter Plumbing and Drain Service has eliminated the disgusting and degrading job. (The caste system of social and economic segregation had its origins in ancient India. Four classes or varna ranged from the upper Brahmins or priests to the lower Sudras or laborers. The system implicitly had a fifth category, those deemed completely outside its scope, the impure or untouchable caste. Although outlawed by Articles 15 and 17 of the Constitution of India, discrimination based on caste and the practice of untouchability exists in twenty-first-century India. HPH III)

Tower of Silence

I met up with a cab driver who belonged to one of the world's great religions, Zoroastrianism, sometimes called Parsee. They worship two supreme beings, Ahura Mazda, manifestation of the light, and Angra Mainyu, manifestation of the dark, through the four basic elements, earth, air, fire, and water. A devout Parsee will not smoke because it despoils fire; he will not drink alcohol, since it is not water; he will not contaminate the earth and air by leaving rubbish or garbage to rot and pollute. A beautiful and clean discipline.

But what does one do with a dead Parsee? Can't burn him as the Hindus do—a diseased body would contaminate both fire and air. Can't bury or burn him as the Christians do—contaminates fire and earth. Can't chuck him into the nearest river—sacrilege to water. Thus, the eerie towers of silence!

My self-appointed guide took me out to the edge of the city to a park with temples and tall, unusual trees—unusual, because their major limbs were bare halfway out from the trunk and polished as smooth as a well-worn stair banister. In the center of the park complex stood a squat, circular tower with no windows and one iron-studded door. The grooved roof appeared to slope inward to an open well. And that was that.

While we were there, a funeral was in progress. Mourners carried a white, cloth-wrapped corpse from a nearby temple, down a path, and through the iron door that screeched with just the proper ethereal touch for the bizarre scene that followed.

The silent procession carried the body to the roof of the tower and immediately returned to the ground, carefully closing the inner-sanctum-sound-effects door. With that as a signal, scores of vultures dropped out of the trees and began to devour the corpse in a startling matter of moments. Soon, nothing remained but bare, white bones. The birds then fluttered on ungainly wings back to the bare branches to await the next dead Parsee, which explained the polished tree limbs. I learned that an average adult would disappear in about twenty minutes and a child in five.

My astonishment didn't end there. The practice honored fire, water, earth, and air, but what about the clean, white bones? The ancient designers of the unique tower of silence had figured that out, too. In rainy, humid, tropical heat, bones soon disintegrated and washed off the grooved roof into a central pit. The pit, actually a filter made of sand and limestone, had four underground pipes leading from its center. I learned that each pipe led precisely north, south, east, and west when the tower was built shortly after the Parsees left Asia Minor some fifteen hundred years before. Rainwater that carried off remains of bones passed through the filter, and the last vestige of our dead Parsee resulted in a crystal-clear glass of potable water. Fabulous and ingenious, but I think it will never replace the muted organ music and banks of flowers at Dawson's Funeral Parlor.

Burning Ghats

Speaking of funerals, I also went to see a Hindu ceremony at the burning ghats. I had no guide, so I never did understand the significance of the detailed procedures. Mourners brought the cloth-covered body to a pyre of logs piled on a wide stone shelf inside a crowded temple area. This Lincoln-Log structure measured about six feet long, three feet wide, and four feet high. After the body was carefully put in place, the widow sprinkled a white powder over the shrouded corpse, the pyre, and, unintentionally, the spectators. All the while, she held a facecloth over her head and moaned, wept, and chanted to her god. Long ago, it was not unusual for a grieving wife to throw herself into the roaring flames.

Officiants carefully escorted a sacred flame from some place I did not see and supervised the lighting of the funeral pyre. As crackling flames spread, mourners increased their volume, and awesome chanting took on an almost hypnotic aura of mystery. Those in charge placed more logs atop the body, mourners scattered more powders about, and more people wailed and chanted. After the body disappeared under the last pieces of wood, those in attendance draped flowers on the peak of the wooden mountain.

I was intrigued that there was no odor of burning flesh. Perhaps the powders had something to do with it or the high heat from dry, rapidly burning wood. I don't know the chemistry, but I am sure it also will never replace Dawson's in Boonton, New Jersey.

Suez Canal

A few days' sail across the Indian Ocean, around the tip of the Arabian peninsula, and into the Red Sea, we were on our way from India to Port Said, Egypt, which I learned to pronounce as Say-ed. I was disappointed to learn we would have no shore leave. We next learned immediately by a flash report that we would get time off in Alexandria at the north end of the Suez Canal, a much more cosmopolitan and lively city, anyhow.

Funny thing about shipboard rumors. I don't know about the navy with its "Now-hear-this" intercom system. Back in my days at sea, the captain could think a plan, and it would be repeated as he thought it in the crew's mess, the engine room, and the galley, the three most sensitive message centers on board ship. Latrine rumors are for shoreside landlubbers. As for vessels in the merchant marine, they really don't need bull horns, intercoms, or bulletin boards. A helmsman with big ears, a retentive memory, and a loose tongue does wonders.

Steaming through the Suez Canal, I experienced a peculiar and strange phenomenon. Have you ever had the dry sweats? It worked like this. Out on the hot deck, the sun hammered down, and a hot, dry wind blew off the baked desert. As one worked, sweat flowed out of his pores to evaporate in an instant. You knew you should be wet with sweat, but incredibly, you found yourself dry as a bone. Maybe that's why sun-seared desert natives have skin like well-tanned leather. Maybe the pores close up for good to help the body retain its water.

Cliff and I put one over on a small group of passengers. We told them the Red Sea got its name because the ancient Pharaohs killed so many people, the sea got stained red from the blood. The blood seeped into rocks on the sea floor so that, even today, the water has a reddish tint. One of the passengers got so mad that he was ready to go ashore in Port Said and spit in the eye of the first Egyptian he saw.

Boy, how gullible.

Alexandria

Alexandria lived up to all its advance publicity. The passengers rushed ashore to get fleeced by robed and sandaled merchants; to visit the big hotels; to join much-publicized tours to Cairo, the ancient pyramids, the Sphinx; and to do all the other things

El Faridieh Hotel Alexandria, Egypt, luggage sticker

passengers do like a flock of sheep. We crew members wound up our duties, washed up, put on our easily identified shore clothes, and lit out for the nearest bar that supplied the two basic ingredients required for men who follow the sea:

• a cold, frothy beer at a reasonable price and

• a good looking, friendly girl to help drink it

Sailors seek such a Utopia the world around. When they find such a place, it is like Mr. Sutter at his sluice box, the boon of hydraulic mining. They fondly talk about it for the rest of their lives.

My shipmate and I wandered around a bit and ended up at one of Alexandria's outdoor, umbrella-shrouded cafes. We enjoyed another cold beer when a little fellow no more than nine or ten years old came over and put on a sleight-of-hand show good enough for the Borscht Circuit vaudeville in the Catskills of New York state. For a small tip, he made baby chicks appear out of nowhere, red marbles turn to blue ones right before our eyes, and little rubber peas appear or disappear at will from under little red cups on our table. When the brief but startling show ended, he disappeared as quickly as the baby chicks. I am sure that loose wallets, wrist watches, and fountain pens disappeared with equal ease.

I learned early on to leave my valuables on board when going ashore. We emptied our pockets of everything except some cash of the country we visited and our American seaman's papers. We left wallets, watches, and other valuables in our lockers. I find myself observing the practice on the rare occasion when I find myself adrift in some strange location. Every lawyer, policeman, and good friend will tell you it's the worst thing in the world to do in a strange place. Maybe so, but I have yet to have my pocket picked or watch removed from my wrist.

Pit Boss

Alexandria offered a hidden advantage introduced to me by a knowledgeable and experienced steward. Eastbound crews from Italy heading through the canal to the Orient have leftover francs and lira they will swap for rupees or Singapore dollars, so a shrewd bargainer can build up a discounted fortune. Also, illegal yet professional money exchangers will do the same thing, giving much better exchange rates than the banks. Having not spent much of my tips or pay in those strange Oriental ports, I had quite a lot of American dollars that expanded overnight into a veritable fortune. Most seamen have an unquenchable and driving desire to spend money as fast as they collect it. So on the run across the Mediterranean to Genoa, Italy, a full scale crap game inevitably got started. Gambling with cheap, plentiful lira felt like rolling for cigar coupons.

With so much money floating around, some heated squabbles and fights inevitably broke out concerning who covered what with how much. I had a reputation for being a reasonably honest fellow, so it ended up with me selected as the undisputed pit boss. A couple of rules: my word was final and, since I could no longer shoot, I would take a small cut of each pot. All agreed, and the fights stopped. The game went so well, they wouldn't let me quit. As each watch came off duty, new rollers filled in the spots deserted by crew members going back on duty or who had finally run through their bankroll. My mates filled my tour as bell captain, and actually, no one ever notices bellmen, anyway. So I stayed at the back of the dice table, settling disputes and skimming a little profit from each pot.

The game was honest. We spread a blanket over a chow table, used a bench on its side as a backboard, and stretched a small piece of line across the table about a foot out from the backboard. The roll did not count unless the dice hit the backboard and bounded over the rope. Winners then collected, losers shouted "Let's go," and I picked up a few more lira as I refereed the payoffs. By morning, the game ended, and we headed into Genoa—and I honestly believe I was the richest crew member on board.

Genoa

Genoa was no Camelot, but it felt like a beautiful Garden of Eden after those pathetic Oriental sights and smells. In no time at all, I sat in a posh restaurant eating a gourmet meal that I washed down with delicious Italian wine, all paid for many times over by my crap-shooting shipmates.

Hotel Britannia & Suisse, Genoa, Italy, luggage sticker

Several of us went on a tourist-style tour of the city. Among the sites we visited was Staglieno Cemetery, called Campo Bello or beautiful field, a cemetery more like a museum than a burial ground. Sculptured marble tombs and statues so jammed together that it looked like a huge jumble of surplus left over from the Metropolitan Museum of Art in New York. A statistic-spouting guide told us the number of individual statues, how many millions of lira they had cost over the years, and how crowded it had become so that people were being buried standing on end to conserve space.

I don't remember any of the grisly figures, but I do recall one unique memorial, a spectacular statue of a young man dressed à la Lindbergh with a flying suit composed of riding britches and boots, a civilian-style tunic complete with flowing scarf, and a leather flying helmet with goggles pushed up on the pilot's forehead. That young aviator holds a broken blade propeller. All the artistic symbolism cost the boy's family their life savings, according to the guide, to perpetuate the memory of their young hero killed while shooting up an Ethiopian village during Italy's invasion of that land of cattle herders. I couldn't help but wonder if he had flown into a well-aimed feather spear.

Every good seaman soon learns to recognize his own ship's whistle. Even in a busy harbor alive with swarming tugs, lighters, pleasure craft, tankers, tour boats, and freighters, each hoot, tweet, screech, wail, and honk has its own personal and recognizable voice. An hour or so before sailing time, the *Harrison* always bellowed a deep resonant h-o-o-o-t so that both crew and passengers knew to come aboard as quickly as possible. I mention it so that you'll appreciate the next episode in its fullness.

The Stroll

Cliff and I had decided to spend some of my crap table earnings on a Saturday night binge. A westernized port, Genoa had clean restaurants, recognizable food, pretty girls, and familiar sights, sounds, and smells. We put on our shoreside clothes and headed for the big square in the middle of Genoa. We had heard that, if an afternoon stroll around the square did not produce results, we might as well give up the whole idea and go to a movie. We taxied to the square and, sure enough, there strolled what looked like half of Italy. The trick, we heard, was to walk against the tide and look over the oncoming traffic. After a couple of laps, the field could be narrowed down and serious trolling could begin.

Pretty soon, our bait was taken, and after a few friendly smiles, we walked four in hand in the same direction—which led to a nearby sidewalk cafe, then a restaurant, and finally an apartment. Saturday night was a steady round of talking, eating, and wine. We got spoiled rotten, and we loved every minute of it. Sunday morning, our companions served us breakfast in bed. By that time, we were convinced that Italy had the best food, best wine, and best girls and qualified as the best shore-leave port in the entire world.

Then we heard, through the din of clanging church bells and church-going traffic, the long, demanding h-o-o-o-t of our ship's whistle. We flew out of bed, tried to explain to our startled hostesses why we suddenly had come to life like that, and scrambled for the stairway. On the way out, we thanked our friends profusely for their great hospitality and offered to help pay for the food and drink they had so graciously provided. We almost fell headlong down the rest of the stairs when they laughingly told us they wouldn't accept a thing, since they normally did the same thing all the time for money. They had decided while walking around the park that they would take a holiday for the weekend—and we qualified as the holiday.

Some holiday!

Going Ashore Box

As we rushed across the square past a busily thronged church, Cliff dropped his going-ashore box, a cigar box he carried with him on shore leave that contained just about everything he felt he would need while indulging in his favorite pastime. His unique first-aid kit contained a variety of rubber contraceptives, Vaseline, several special medications, their unique applicators, and, to use a polite term, two or three different kinds of insect repellents. He had a veritable venereal disease clinic under his arm.

Disaster struck. Cliff stumbled on a curb, and the box went flying. A crowd of well-dressed churchgoers circled around and applauded as Cliff scrambled to pick up his scattered and easily recognizable valuables. Having collapsed in a heap on the curb and reduced to total inactivity by uncontrollable gales of side-splitting laughter, I provided absolutely no help. Cliff never let me forget that I had let him down when he needed a shipmate's help the most.

Marseilles

From Genoa, we steamed on to Marseilles, France. By then, the war had gotten serious. The captain had huge American flags painted on two hatch covers and on both sides of our vessel. We kept them floodlit all night to help trigger happy U-boat captains and aerial bomb sighters to know that we sailed as American neutrals and not British war trophies to be hung over the Fuehrer's fireplace.

On that run, we heard a story that bears repetition. One of our crew was a young, red-headed, fiery-tempered midwesterner whose political leanings bent toward Moscow. At sea, a man's personal life is his own matter, and he is left alone with it. If he wants to talk about personal things, that's up to him. You don't ask questions.

Hôtel de la Poste, Marseille(s), France, luggage sticker

Red talked. He told of how he went to Spain and joined the Loyalist Abraham Lincoln Brigade, a Communist-backed group of soldiers of fortune. He told of fighting against the Fascists trained by the Hitler and Mussolini military. Red's hatred for German and Italian troops was unreal. Wounded, he had returned to the states just before signing on with us. His wounds were partly mental. When he talked excitedly about the war, he cursed the Nazis and Italians and got so overwrought that he actually drooled at the corners of his mouth. We got to know that signal meant leave him alone.

Knowing what we did about Red, I can believe the rest of the story. When we left Genoa, Red was not with us. The "shipboard telegraph" said he had taken on a load of wine, met some Italian veterans of the Spanish War, and proceeded to tell them what he thought of Italy, Italians in general, and Mussolini in particular. Up to then, he was only in the normal trouble that any shoreside sailor might find himself. But curse El Duce and you could find yourself in deep, festering trouble. In fact, Red had disappeared. Pleas to the Polizia, the American consul, and other authorities turned up no Red. Help was in the works, but the ship could not be held up for one missing crew member. I never heard what happened to our shipmate, but knowing how fanatic he was about anything Fascist, I have a pretty good idea that the key was thrown away.

After Genoa, Marseilles proved a very sad bust. I don't remember much about it except that it was full of black market merchants trying to sell cigarettes, liquor, and whatever. The war had just started, and those noble citizens lost no time in getting to work. I remember seeing a sign on a storefront that said "1,000,000 chemises." I idly wondered if French girls even wore chemises anymore, let alone how do you sell a million of them. I was soon advised that in France a chemise is a shirt—not a female undergarment.

Heading Home

Well, that was that. A short run through Gibraltar under the watchful and protective eye of the Royal Navy, and we were on our way to New York and home. Only there did I learn that, all through the Orient, the Suez, the Mediterranean, and the North Atlantic, we had constituted an inviting sitting duck. Hidden among our dry cargo had been a reputed eleven million dollars in gold bullion, cash payment from free China for equipment, supplies, and arms for the Chennault Flying Tigers. (Claire L. Chennault, retired US Army Air Corps officer, military aviation advisor to Generalissimo Chiang Kai-shek of China, helped form the Flying Tigers, a group of volunteer American military pilots who served as part of the Chinese Air Force in World War II. HPH III)

In New York, I paid off for the last time and headed home. I had a bag full of souvenirs—stuff I'd bought, bargained, traded, and bluffed away from all sorts of places, each of little value other than the stories connected with it.

I was anxious to see if I could persuade the folks at General Foods that they needed me. In all the millions of years that the world has been going around, there has been only one me, and General Foods sure can't let an opportunity like that slip by—*two* Haldts with them would be their making.

As I said goodbye to the sea, I remembered a story allegedly told by an old-time, square-rigger sailor. He said he was going to put a pair of oars over his shoulder and head inland. If and when someone stopped him to ask, "Hey, Mister, what are them things?" he'd drop his anchor right there and raise chickens.

I didn't do that. I stepped on board the merry-go-round, got a job, got married, had kids, and lived happily ever after. Now here I am, retired and living in Florida, with wonderful and exciting memories of my days as a youth on deepwater vessels.

THE TIMES-BULLETIN

BOONTON, N. J., TUESDAY, OCTOBER 31, 1939. CHARLES L. GRUBB, Editor

H. Peale Haldt Tells of Experiences On a 'Round-the-World' Trip

This letter was received this week and was dated Wednesday, September 27, 1939, en route Suez, Egypt, from H. Peale Haldt, Vreeland avenue, Boonton:

When I left on this 'round-the-world trip last July I promised that you should get a letter from me. If, after you have read it, you still want to use it you are perfectly welcome to it—so here goes:

Naturally the thing uppermost in the news today is this fracus they are pulling off in Europe. The Orient feels this strain, too. The steamer I'm working on has hit British ports all along the line where war activities are under full swing. But our personal experiences began before Hitler said "Boo!" to Poland. In the crowded harbor of Manila we picked up a cargo of Chinese gold to aid in her struggle with Japan. Our forward hold has just under $3,000,000 in gold stowed away. In Manila we heard the announcement that war had been declared. Naturally three millions in any kind of gold is quite a haul. Therefore we pussy-footed our way from then on with visions of another neutral ship with a torpedo hole in it.

In Singapore our ship was led in the "back door," a narrow channel usually reserved as the exit from their wharfs. We were told later that this unusual procedure was necessary as the main entrance was heavily mined. As it was, gunboats watched us closely and a conversation with a Scotch Highlander later pointed out that several batteries of guns were trained on us as we steamed in. Reserve troops were pouring in to take over the many military duties. The town itself was on the verge of being under martial law. Blockade runners painted a dull black from bow to stern, truck to keel were loading food supplies, guns, and other war materials to take to various out-of-the-way army posts. Troop ships stood by, sand bags around her more vulnerable spots and a newly mounted gun on her stern. The busy port even had 'black outs' in preparation for some serious trouble. Strangely what they fear the most is an open war with Japan. In that case Singapore will be a mighty important key position.

But Bombay, India, was the most unreal port we have hit. There the war was something that only the hated Limies were concerned with. To the natives their freedom was the immediate question. Perhaps the word "hated" sounds strong to you. Actually that is the case. Through education that the English have instituted, the natives realize that they are taking an awful kicking. Now they are waiting to see what the mother country has to say as a result of the present conflict. They feel that if England will allow them a separate government in which they can rule themselves, they will help England in

(Continued on Page Four)

EDWARD J. CAHILL AGENCY
Mary C. Ginder, Manager
Fire and Casualty Insurance
710 Main Street   Boonton, N. J.
Telephone Boonton 8-0166

Peale's account of October 31, 1939, of his world tour aboard SS President Harrison as published in the Boonton, New Jersey, Times-Bulletin

Page Four

H. Peale Haldt Tells of Experiences

(continued from page one)

her fight. If the boys at the House of Parliament refuse this request the natives warn that they will have more than the German Nazis to worry about.

But aside from the war question, we saw some things that are usually only read about. For example, the forbidding Towers of Silence. Here on a lonely hilltop the 50,000 Pursees in Bombay have five ancient stadium-like towers about 20 feet high and 100 feet across. In them they leave their dead to be eaten by ugly but thorough vultures. The Pursees, driven from Persia several thousand years ago, came to India with their religion based on the All Master, their supreme being. He is worshipped through nature, their methods being through the mediums of fire, air, earth and sun. They don't smoke, as that would be a sacrilege to the fire; they don't bury their dead as that would make the earth unclean. Therefore the vultures. As one goes into the grounds the fluttering of the wings of the heavy birds can be heard in the trees, on the temple roofs, even on the edge of the towers as though hungrily awaiting another meal. The Hindus, an even older religion, have a different method of disposing with the dead.

In one section of town, backed by the tram car barn, are the burning ghats. Here in what seems to be a small alleyway, the Hindu dead are none too carefully placed on a bier of wood. A relative and a holy man sets fire to it and lets nature do the rest. When we came in there were three or more bodies spread stiffly on the ground awaiting their turn. When they saw our cameras they invited us past the spot where visitors have to stop so that we were standing within ten feet of the dead. Although cameras were strictly forbidden, they asked us to use the movie camera. Gladly I did, though not adding that I had been sneaking pictures all the while.

"Now watch," our self-appointed guide said. "See, they pick up the body, always careful to keep that cloth between the dead man's skin and their hands. Now see that man with the burning stick?" We watched a young Hindu take a small faggot from the fire, touch the protruding foot, walk around the bier and repeat the operation. "That is the son. He does that for it is an old, old custom. He does it seven times, muttering prayers all the time. Now see the flames eat higher. Soon there will be nothing but ashes." We had the feeling that it was some kind of a side show trick. It almost seemed that after we had gone, the "body" got up, collected his fee and waited for the next showing. But we knew it was real. The burning flesh, that horror of watching the protruding leg blacken and burn was no trick. It was real. Too damned real for us so we

en and burn was no trick. It was real. Too damned real for us so we ... ... accepting the invitation to stay and watch them cremate a little girl that had died of malnutrition.

Once in the open air we looked sheepishly at each other, not admitting that either felt squeamish, but knowing that we both did. My partner, Cliff Beckwith of the Ozarks, and I, headed back to the ship wondering if maybe the world was wrong and these Hindus with their castes, their cremations and the myriad other unusual customs were right.

One little bit of humor to end this letter with. The other night we went ashore to see the Mohammedan section of town where the women still wear veils. As we were both track men of sorts we got into an argument as to who could run the faster. Then and there we decided to have a race. The time, 2:30 A. M. The place, a dark street somewhat alive with people on their way to some place or other. We picked a street light two blocks down the line. We started out at a great clip, only a few natives wondering what was wrong. About half way to the light we were neck and neck, legging it as fast as we thought we could. Then out came a dog as big as a wolf. I didn't even look at it. All I know is that I passed Cliff like he was going the other way, passed the light and got half way into the dock area before I realized that the "wolf" was miles behind. Probably dead from exhaustion—I hope! I won the bet but for a while I thought I'd never be able to use it.

Now we are heading for the Mediterranean Sea, "war zone," with flags all over our ship. Maybe I will be telling you how it feels to be torpedoed. Till then,

Sincerely,
PEALE HALDT.

Peale working the lines on board Sea Cloud, *1983*

Join Me While I Peel Off Forty-Six Years
an epilogue written on April 10, 1983 by H. Peale Haldt Jr.

Sea Cloud

1937 and 1983

The ginseng root has its disciples, the 1890 fifty-cent bottle of magic elixir revitalized many a believer, and the fabled monkey gland extract still has its wide-eyed adherents. I, however, just experienced having the years peeled off me like the growth layers of a huge Florida onion.

Join me while I peel off forty-six years.

We find a young college student working as an able-bodied seaman on the brand new, shiny black barque, *Sea Cloud*, the private yacht and pride and joy of Ambassador Joseph E. Davies and his wife, Marjorie Merriweather Post, heiress to the General Foods fortune. I had wrangled an early release from Colgate University in 1937 so I could sail on her into the Baltic and on to Russia. When I joined up with her, she was barely six years old. Her brass shone like gold as did the faucets in the master bath, since they were gold. Her teak decks sparkled like snow, the result of regular washdowns by the crew—including me. Her varnish gleamed from constant sanding and revarnishing. Her twenty-nine sails, when billowed with a following wind, confirmed her name—she was indeed a beautiful, stately cloud.

As a foredeck hand living in the fo'c'sle, I had relatively simple duties. Since she was new, she was easy to care for. Simple maintenance with polishing cloth, sandpaper, varnish, and Clorox kept us busy while in port or at anchor. Climbing the rigging, furling or unfurling the heavy canvas sails, and working the lines from the deck while underway kept us busier still. And Mrs. Davies loved to see her *Sea Cloud* heeled over with a stiff quartering wind bellying her sails. So did the crew.

Back then, about seventy-two people made up the crew. Running the ship were the captain, three mates, a bo'sun, a

guest patch and shaving of deck teak for a "former crew mate" from 1983 Sea Cloud *windjammer cruise Peale took with his wife, Barbara*

quartermaster, radioman or Sparks, the deck gang, and the black or engineering gang. To accommodate the needs of the Davieses and guests, the stewards department—including chefs, assistant cooks, waiters, room maids, hairdressers, storekeepers, and private secretaries—took care of them in style.

In February, 1983 I once again stood on the rolling deck of that beautiful ship. At that precise moment, I saw and felt the onion layers peel away. Ponce de Leon never found his magic water, but I did that very first day. My wife had booked a Caribbean cruise for us but had neglected to tell me anything about the ship. As I stood on that deck and took it all in, I knew why. A tear came to my eye.

The ship had aged forty-six years. Like all beautiful ladies, she had begun to show her age. Nevertheless, once again I stood on the not-quite-so-white teak deck looking aloft at the straining canvas sails topped off by the upper tops'ls and royals. Today, however, she is a different ship. New deck houses or containers, as Captain Edward D. Cassidy calls them, have been added to make her into the windjammer cruise ship she is today. Her new crew, very much like the crew I knew, includes young people from England, Germany, Scandinavia, the USA, and the Far East. Instead of the seventy-two crewmen I knew, they now have some fifty crewpersons. What a pleasant but startling surprise to see young ladies hauling the lines, scraping paint, and climbing the rigging right along with the men. They were hard workers, dedicated to the ship—and very pretty!

I must pin medals on each and every one of the ship's hardworking crew. Those people are actually rebuilding the *Sea Cloud* right under our feet. Fifty-odd years of sailing as a private yacht, declining as a floating headquarters for a construction company, and finally left to die a pauper's death at a desolate Panamanian dock left deep scars. Under her new management, she has been brought back to life. Now Captain Cassidy and his expert crew are doing the impossible—wiping away the wrinkles and grime and letting her former beauty gleam once again.

In those olden days of the 1930s, we had stock answers for the curious sightseer who would look aloft and ask the inevitable question, "Golly! How much rope does this boat have?"

"We have about twenty-five feet of rope—and about twenty-five miles of line."

Or, "Isn't it scary working way up there in the sails?"

"Not bad. We just keep our eyes closed until we get used to it."

Or, "Do you fellows ever get seasick?"

"All the time. It's part of being a sailor."

Oh, for those good old days.

If I sound a bit romantic and mushy about that ship, please bear with me. I don't apologize for being in love with her. If you ever have the opportunity to sail on her, I hope you will be able to do so and enjoy the thrill of being a part of the last of the great privately owned square riggers.

Sea Cloud, *1995, with deck cabins added for cruise passengers, including Peale and Barbara in 1983*

COMPARISON OF SHIP CHARACTERISTICS

	Ringfond	*George B. Cluett*	*Sea Cloud*	*President Harrison*
built	Leirvik, Norway	Tottenville, Staten Island, New York	Kiel, Germany	Camden, New Jersey
year	1901	1911	1931	1920
displacement in tons	603	210	3,530	10,509
length in feet	171	135	316	502
beam in feet	28	26	49	62
draft in feet	15	12	16	28
speed in knots	7	5.5	12	14

transcriptions from entries in Peale's logbooks

transcription of *Ringfond* log, inside front cover on page 8

Ship. *RINGFOND*
Bound for-Hayti

Ship's officers
Captain-Stian E. Brinch
1st Mate-Eav Eliasson
2nd Mate-Nardal Emil Olsen
Chief Engineer-Eilert Johnsson
Steward-O. Bjorn
Third Engineer-Runert Baardsen

We have three cats on board: Hans, Siri, plus Unknown. Hans is a freak. He has seven claws on his two front paws and five on the rest.

Ringfond log, page 1 • Thursday, June 4, 1931 on page 9

First entry

Thursday 4, 1931

Left Hoboken on ship *Ringfond*. Picked up pilot at dock at Franklin Baker Coconut Co. Shoved off at about 7:30. Passed Coney Island at 9:05. We have full privileges on the ship, fore—aft and all over. Captain showed us around the ship. Dropped pilot at about 9:36. The boat is taking the swells swell. Good night till tomorrow.

Friday 5, 1931

We didn't sleep very well last nite. The watch was out there and we went out about 1:00 AM. Later Captain Brinch, pronounced Brinch, came out. Gee, he's a swell guy, no kiddin'. About 7:30 we sighted an old oil tanker and a steamer of the United Fruit Co. We just came back from a stroll around the ship. Haven't sighted land since last nite. Saw a bunch of porpoises. Ran for our cameras. Sun was under the cloud but still we tried. The school passed within about 20 ft of the stern but our camera finger wasn't swift enuf to get the picture. Sorry to disappoint you. Well, at last, Mt. Peale erupted. Boy. Was I sick some spuds, ink, small nails etc are all fish food now.

Saturday 6, 1931
    Tom admits that he's pretty green around the gills but I know he is better. I have been so since around one o'clock AM. Passed Cape Henry Light house about 5:45 and picked up pilot at some place about a quarter of a mile from shore.

Ringfond log page 19 • Saturday July 4, 1931 on page 9

Porridge.
Read till evening had a small meal. Went up forward & played Fan Tan. Went to bed about 8:30.

    Saturday. Woke up dreaming that I was drowning but found out that rain was coming in the port hole and I was soaked. I was so tired that I didn't feel like getting up but a big clap of thunder changed my mind for me. It was raining "cats & dogs" but I couldn't find any. I put on my slicker and was standing by the rail holding it when WHAM !!!boy !!The lightning struck the water and the ship at the same time. My mouth felt like I swallowed a quart of battery juice, my hands were tingling and I was scared. After that the rain eased up a bit and so I went up on the bridge. The Stevensons gave me a big bunch of bananas and when the lightning hit them they all turned yellow and are now almost over ripe. Stayed up on the bridge a while and the chief mate took an observation, so did I. My answer was 2° out of the way. Later the 2nd mate did the same and I was 3° out this time.

Ringfond log page 38 • Wednesday July 22, 1931 on page 10

    Wednesday. Woke up 7:00. Went down to the steward till 8:00. Had breakfast at 8:30. Came up on the bridge till 10:00. Went aft and talked with the Chief. Stayed there till noon. During that morning 6 ships have passed us. Had dinner at 12:30. Came up on bridge till 4:00. Was watching the other ships thru the glass (binoculars, HPH III) and passed 3 more ships. Went down in the engine room till 5:00. Went down in saloon (crew mess or eating place, HPH III) till 6:30. Ate dinner. 6:45. Went down into the boiler room till 8:30. Boy, that's a very nice little place to play in. There you stand with nothing on except pants, shoes and a pair of gloves. The three hot furnaces are blazing with the refreshing heat of 200 degrees F right in front of you. The bunkers of soft, fine, and "much a dirty" coal on both sides and you stand there shoveling that same matter into the mouths of those ever-hungry furnaces at the rate of 25,600 ounces per two hours with an ordinary iron shovel that has a wooden handle. When you stop working you have to sit on a stack of blotters because you perspire so readily you might fill up the bilges (bottom of the hull where water collects, HPH III) faster than the bilge pump can get it out and that would end with a disastrous result.

Cluett log front page on page 32

Private Log of Peale Haldt 1934
1. Private log page 1
2. Officers and crew 104
3. Diagrams and drawings 105
4. Miles and hours 116
5. Official log 117
6. Bit of a sea yarn 121
7. To be read while waiting for mail 126
8. Sea Songs and others 127

Cluett log page 37 • July 22, 1934 on page 31

Sunday 22nd 10:00 PM

A bit of excitement today. We all put on the glad rags, piled into a dory and headed for the church. The only church here and the minister was away so we headed for the opposite shore to the mission. There we stayed until noon, talking and reading. After dinner some went ashore but two of us stayed on board and read. I slept a bit, too. At four o'clock we rowed ashore just in time to see the sandwich plate empty. We did get a cookie or two and a splash of tea. I came back and climbed up in the topmost bed to read. From the sound of that you'd think it was rum or something I had instead of tea. I was reading the Strand Magazine, printed in England. Tom and I got our dinner tonight. We had toasted cheese sandwich, fried spuds, After dinner I was aft reading some of the skipper's books when we decided to go up in the airplane. It costs $2.50 for 10 minutes. 6 of us—one the skipper, all flew for about 15 minutes. At one time we were 2,500 ft. high and at another time we hit 120 mph. It was a Fairchild sea plane owned by the Canadian Airways Limited. The only trouble is I'm broke now and won't be able to buy that Eskimo dickie. Hope there's some kale at St. Anthony.

Cluett log page • July 27, 1934 on page 37

Friday, July 27th

A bit more working today. We finished dodging between the rain drops and when, after dinner, we finished unloading we had to wash down the decks. That was fun. I rolled up my trousers and went barefooted. Down came the "Loon," a small motor sailer, towing a barge load of lumber about 10—20 ft. long and thick as your leg. We stayed down there until dark, unloaded 573 chunks. When we finished, the five of us who were down in the hold went in swimming. I made about 8 dives and had about 10 minutes of good, cold swimming. Then came the fun! I was the last down the companionway so I had to clean up. I stepped on a cake of soap, did not slip but when I started down the wet companionway—well, I don't know quite what happened but I was very suddenly at the bottom with a crack on the back of my head. The nurse at the hospital fixed it up but asked me to come tomorrow and get it fixed good. Another fellow got a small bear skin, easily worth the $11 he payed for it. If only I had my mail—perhaps there'd be some money in it (there'd better be or—or—well, just plain or).

Cluett log page 83 • September 4, 1934 on page 39

Tuesday Sept 4th

Believe it or not—I'm eighteen.

To commemorate this fact, I had a sort of Birthday party at midnight. Under the circumstances the chances of my receiving any presents being very slim I gave presents away instead. I had some cookies left over so everyone in our watch got some.

Later in the morning we began to plod into really heavy weather. The Cluett dug her bow into the seas that were slowly hauling around to our bow so that by noon we were driving head on into the seas. It's days like this that the cook doesn't have to prepare much food.

In the evening the mates watch was feeling pretty low and by this time only a few of us have recovered (meaning two out of three—I, luckily being one of the two).

We are somewhere off Cape Ray as I write at midnight and won't come to the Gut for a day or so.

I traded Dickie Paeldon some chocolate, gum & 10 cents for a hat of his. It's pretty good and I still don't know which of us lost.

This evening the stars are shining for the first time in many a week so we do have some hope left for us.

Sea Cloud log page 15 • June 11, 1937 on page 60

Thursday, June 11th

Several days ago we were in Kiel. There we were to go into dry dock and have our bottom (the ship of course) scraped. The dock broke down and so we had to sail for Stettin where a larger dock could be obtained. Kiel is too navy minded. Everybody either has a uniform or they are women. All the shipyards have navy boats in them and we just didn't rate. One Saturday when the port watch had liberty we wore our work uniforms ashore to rent kayaks and go canoing. On the way to the club we were besieged by autograph hounds who, when we had our shore clothes on, paid no attention to us. However, with the faintest suggestion of uniforms we were the Cock of the Walk. The paddle-boating was indeed fun. When we came back, we were soaked but gleaming with the sport of it.

Another time six of us were passing a second hand shop window when a pile of old high hats caught our eye. In less than five minutes we were all be-hatted and one mark less. A high-topper for 25¢. Some fun, eh!

Sea Cloud log page 27 • July 9 and 15, 1937 on page 77

Even the Russian who lives in the city can not leave unless he possesses a pass. Nice place, eh? In Moscow, I read, they are shooting men left and right for treason, spying and blowing the Trans-Siberian Railway eighty feet off the ground . . . No Sir! Not for me . . . I'll do as the poets suggest and be a Scowegian.

Thursday, July 15
Again a lot of water has splashed against our sides since the last time. Since then we have gone in more for social work than sight-seeing. Our first stop was Götenburg, Sweden but my job as launch-man made it impossible for me to go ashore. While waiting for the owners' party I had a chance to leave the launch and see a little bit of the town but not all I wanted to. Later we went to the King's summer home and he rode in our launch. King Gus is really quite a lad. Seventy-some years old and still playing tennis. (King Gustav V, seventy-nine years old at the time, was king from 1907 to 1950. HPH III)

Sea Cloud log page 28 • July 15, 1937 on page 78

While riding in, he had his legs crossed and was picking pebbles from his shoe as no ordinary old man could do without breaking six or seven bones. His royal highness was accompanied by the Mr. & Mrs. Crown Prince. While on board he was sung to by none other than Lawrence Tibbet who is also a guest on our ship. He and his wife came on in Götenburg and are still here. Last nite he gave another "practice session" in which we were allowed to listen. All I can say was he was marvelous and even better than his reputation. (Lawrence Tibbett, 1896-1960, was a famous American opera singer. HPH III).

Again we moved. This time to Copenhagen the land of snuff—or rather where snuff got it's name but funny, it's not made there. I got someone to stand my job in the launch and went ashore with the bo'sun. A short evening but I saw enuf of Copenhagen to want to live there when I grow old. Quiet, clean, beautiful; all that one would want. A toast to Denmark. But this is overshadowed by a return trip to Leningrad! Boo!!

Sea Cloud log page 11 • May 19, 1937 on page 86

I'm at last beginning to feel the part I'm trying to act—that of a canvas sailor. My blisters have slowly changed to callouses and I'm getting used to the four hour on-and-off plan. All that remains is to get used to the weather. The night look-outs on the forecastle head are killers. Spray comes up and you'd swear it freezes on you. That, of course, depends on the imagination powers.

Tuesday 24th

At last, the brightly painted boat has gouged a hole for itself in Kiel harbor. But that's a little ahead of the story. Wednesday last, the Queen Mary slid past us taking all of fifteen minutes to come into and pass out of our sights. I wanted to take some movies but it was a little too far away. We were still rolling quite a bit yet she seemed to feel them but little.

The weather has been clearing up quite a bit tho and Sunday we had a fair breeze. Thru the channel it was of course quite foggy. "Patches of mist . . ." as the radio announcer . . . .

Experiencing What My Father Did
a postscript by Captain Harry Peale Haldt III, United States Navy (retired)

As a young officer in the navy, I had the opportunity to experience some of the same sights and smells that my father did on his 'round-the-world trip on the *President Harrison*. I was in my early twenties, about the same age.

I had two deployments on board USS *Tripoli* (LPH-10) between 1969 and 1971 that got me to Hawaii, Japan, Hong Kong, and Manila, all ports that my father visited and writes about in his journals.

I walked on the sands of Waikiki Beach in Honolulu and sat on the veranda of the Royal Hawaiian Hotel, but I did not go surfboarding.

I experienced the ritual of a Japanese bathhouse in Naha, Okinawa, Japan, and found it just as my father related in his story. I never got to Yokohama or Tokyo but did get into Sasebo, a Japanese port city on the southern tip of Honshu Island. As a souvenir, I brought home a pachinko game, a combination slot machine and pinball game.

In Hong Kong, I also got to the top of Victoria Peak, although not by rickshaw. Hong Kong and Kowloon, across the harbor, were still full of shops, street peddlers and smells unknown to me. I did not get a tattoo or a haircut from a horseshoe barber, but I did get some tailor-made shirts and shoes, the most comfortable shoes I ever had. They lasted a very long time.

Tripoli went in and out of Subic Bay, Philippines, many times during those deployments, and I often visited Olongapo City. Anyone who has been there knows those sights and smells are unforgettable!

Anyhow, I also visited the beautiful city of Manila. For sure, the sheds on poles were still there, however. My most memorable recollection of Manila? Getting shaken awake at night in a hotel by an earthquake and evacuating the building.

An Unlikely Correspondence: letters to Peale from Nedenia Hutton, later the movie star Dina Merrill

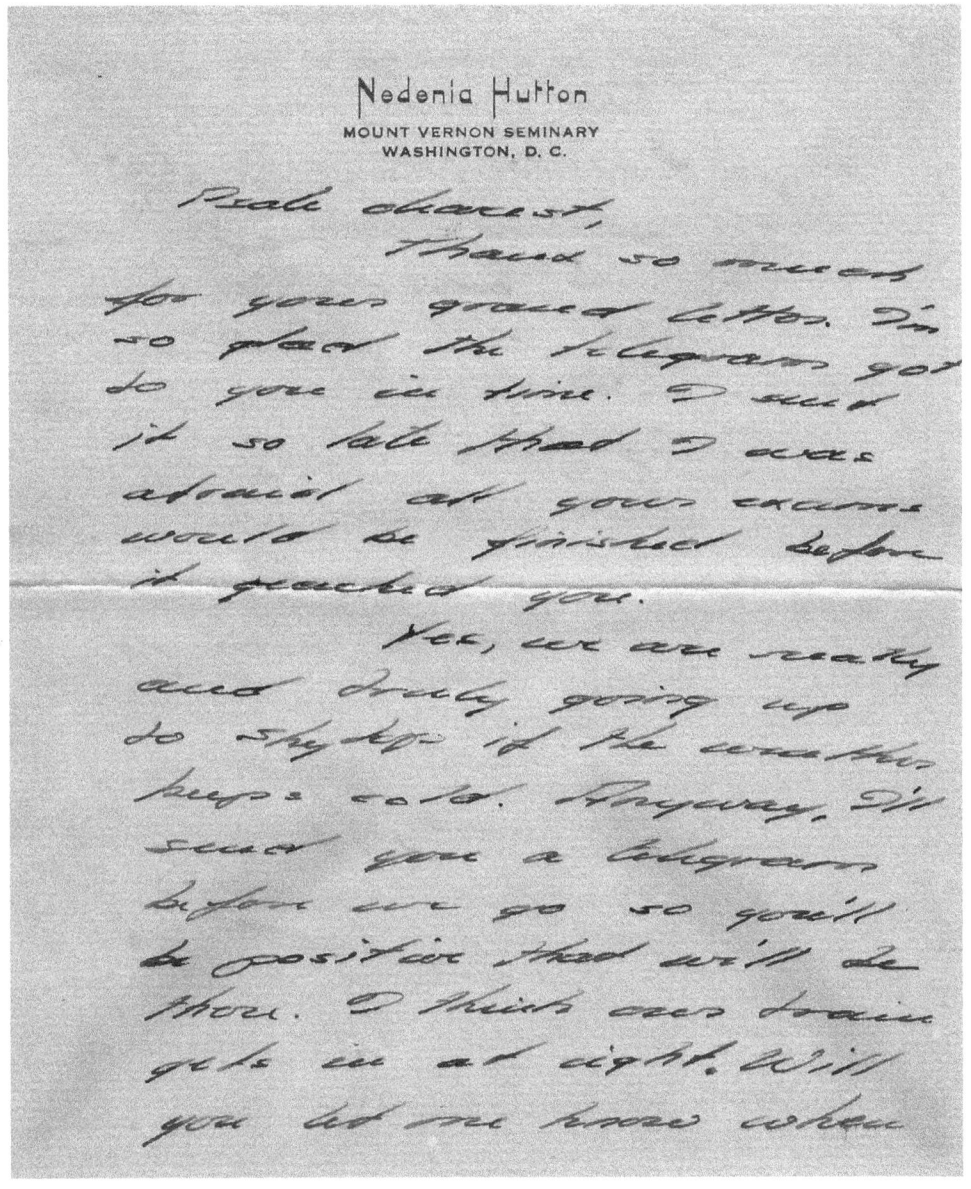

first page of a letter from Nedenia Hutton to Peale, January 30, 1939, continued on the next three pages and then followed by transcriptions of other letters in the correspondence

you'll get there and there we can arrange a place where we can meet you. As to ice-skating, we're both game. Len's has been on them exactly once and I've only been on them 3 or four times, but will try anything once. Honestly, I just can't wait!! It'll be the first time that I've ever been in a place that has a lot of snow and ice. Also, I've only been on skis once and I'm kinda scared of them, but maybe I'll do well (with enough persuasion).

Nedenia Hutton
MOUNT VERNON SEMINARY
WASHINGTON, D. C.

to screw up my courage and try.

I talked to Mummy over the phone yesterday and she said she was going to bring the Sea Cloud over to Belgium in May and she was going up to Russia again. The general opinion is that there will be a war in Europe some time this Spring. If it breaks while the Sea Cloud is over there, she'll be commandeered and that will be the last we'll see of her. I do so wish Mummy would leave well enough alone and leave her sitting safely in Jacksonville. I just couldn't bear to have anything happen to her.

I really should run along and study for that darn 3 hour exam on Wednesday. Wish me luck!!
Love,
Dearie

*Nedenia Hutton
the actress Dina Merrill*

Letters from Nedenia Hutton to H. Peale Haldt Jr.
nineteen letters from May 23, 1938 to May 13, 1939
after operetta practice, Mount Vernon Seminary

May 23, 1938
Peale dearest,

Thanx loads for the two swell letters. I'm 'fraid this one won't live up to either of yours. Reason—I've just come up from a three hour operetta practice and I'm a total wreck. I guess maybe I just can't take it.

Thanx so much for the pledge pin. I'll try to live up to requirements if I can. I'll consider it you in person (great imagination) and I'll try not to do anything *too* awful. I'm not promising tho. It's hard for me to play the little angel.

And now, what's this I hear about you wanting to spank the daylights out of me? Well, well!! You won't try it more than once if I'm still alive and kicking. I'm very sorry you got a cold, but how was I to know that? You don't know how much that meant to me, to see the *Sea Cloud* again. And was I homesick?? Wow!! I've lived many places, but that's the place I call 'home.'

I told Ruth to give Doug a hint about his work. Now, young man, what about you? Where are all those A's? I've got to go wake Ruth up and go to dinner. Poor kid's dead tired and has to act in a French play tonight.

7:15 PM

Well, here we are and this is just an interlude till the kids start coming in to get made up for the play. That's just one disadvantage of taking Dramatic Seminar. Here one comes now. Lord! Not one but three! See you after the play.

2 hrs later

Well, here I am back after seeing three French plays. Little Wallace did herself up brown with the job of being a chef. She really did a very good job of it.

There's a nice little thunderstorm going on now. The foot-lights went out on the stage and somebody dashed off-stage to get a handkerchief and didn't get back on time. It was really very funny.

Anita, one of the dear girls here, is just kidding the life out of me. All I can hear is Jimmie this and Jimmie that. Then, she started kidding Ruth about Doug and I had to stop writing for a few minutes because they chased each other over the bed. If this seems a little messy, t'aint my fault.

Thanx loads for the snap-shots you sent me. How on earth did you ever get the one of my Paw & Maw? (Quote from Anita) I hope she appreciates this!!!

Hope you got the 'special' and won't mind my putting the note in Doug's letter. Think you can make it? I hope so.

I guess the ten o'clock bell did ring half an hour ago, so maybe I ought to hit the hay. (Anita says "darn right I should")

Bye-bye now. Ruth sends her best to you and love to Doug.
Much love,
Deenie

sometime over the summer of 1938
on board *Sea Cloud*

Peale dearest,

I'm so glad you got my wire, tho it's a wonder you did. You see, you forgot to give me any address to answer to! (You would!) Anyway, next time you pass the *Sea Cloud*, come aboard and say 'hello.'

Also, I got your letter today. That trip sounds like grand fun. I'd think you'd get worn out, tho, cycling so much. If I win a bet, I'll be doing quite a little of it. If I lose, I'll have a tennis racquet in my hand all morning for goodness knows how long. While I think of it, do you know if there are three ten-goal polo-players in USA and if one of them is Pete Bostwick? I don't know much about polo, but I have a hunch I'm going to win. Here's hoping, anyway.

From what I hear from Ruth, Doug has been and still is going strong. Also, she told me that he only had one more year to live if he didn't show up. Do you know anything about it? I hope she got something mixed, for her sake. If you see Doug when you get home, give him my best. He seems to be very nice, and Ruth thinks an awful lot of him. I just hope he feels the same way, too. Speaking about beautiful scenes, here's one for you. Just get your imagination oiled up and in good working order, and here we go.

The place is Cardiff, Wales, out in a big lot with trees all 'round. The time is about 9:00 PM and the sky is clear with a few stars showing. The moon is just coming up over the trees and darkness hasn't quite overcome the daylight. Inside the big building, the audience is just taking their seats and a choir of 750 male voices is marching up on the platform. Outside, the crickets are beginning to chirp and an occasional mosquito buzzes by your ear. Just as the moon comes up, the choir starts singing, at first faintly and then with tremendous force. The whole thing was so impressive and beautiful. The choir was one of the most beautiful in the world and the impression was completed by the scenery outside. It was without doubt one of the most enjoyable evenings I have ever spent.

Now, to get back to reality, the *Sea Cloud*. We have only had, as yet, *one* day at sea!! A fine cruise this turned out to be. We were tied up at Ostend for three weeks and then went to Cardiff and stopped at Dover and Southhampton on the way back. I guess it's because Joe doesn't like sailing and being out at sea the way Daddy did. When he was on board, we'd spend half the time under-way and the other half was spent in little tiny towns. No big cities then. It really was loads of fun, tho. We have practically a whole new crew on board. Dodo is still here, and Muller too. Two officers have been changed and the new ones look so much alike I can never tell which is which.

I guess I've been racing on long enough. You're probably sound asleep by now. I hope this gets to you before you leave that place, where-ever it is. Write soon, a nice *long* one.

Much love,
Deenie

On board *Sea Cloud*

Aug. 19, 1938
Peale dear,

Thanx so much for the nice long letter. I'm 'fraid I can't do as well as that, but I'll try.

That information about the polo helped a lot and I won the bet and had a lot of fun cycling over Brussels. Also thanx for telling me about Doug. I wrote Ruth and put her mind at ease on that subject.

We have some guests on board with us now who live in Washington, so I'm getting all the news from them about my friends there. I was told that their daughter who is with them was my age, but she turned out to be eleven. That does me an awful lot of good!

And now, about that coming home proposition. You said to think twice before I decided to stay over here. You know, it wasn't my idea, it was Mother's. She wants me to stay over here till next June and just miss one year of school which I think is a bad idea, but there isn't much I can do about it. You know Mother! If I'm lucky, I may be able to get back in Jan. and go to MVS. I suppose it would be a lot of fun over here, but I'm 'fraid I'd miss all my friends back home. Over here, girls of my age still go around with short socks and big bows in their hair and, of all awful things, pigtails! There is nothing I hate more than pigtails.

When do you plan to sail home? If & when you get home, will you please give my love to Ruth if you happen to see her? Poor kid, she has to go to Dobbs this year. They say that it is one of the strictest boarding schools in the US. I'm afraid poor Ruth will have a hard time after MVS.

I seem to have run very low in material so I guess I'll stop before I utterly collapse. Write soon. Address is always the same. What will yours be?

Much love,
Deenie

from The Plaza Hotel, New York City

Oct. 12, 1938
The Plaza
Fifth Avenue at 59th Street
New York
Peale dearest,

I'm home!! Really and truly home, and I can't quite believe it. It's so wonderful, it just doesn't seem true. I got back yesterday with Mother. We came over on a little tiny boat named the "Duchess of York" and landed in Quebec. We had a horrible trip over and almost everyone was seasick. No, I wasn't, thank goodness. We really did have it rough, tho. The seas came over the bow more than a few times and the wind was terrific. We went at the fast pace of 10 knots for four days running. But assez de a sujet!

You asked me for a picture of me, so here it is! It's only a snap-shot taken on one of the life-boats with the starboard launch in the background. I'm afraid that's the best I can do right now and I hope its OK.

I'm going back to school tomorrow and, I suppose, will settle down to routine again. Quite a change after the wild life I've been leading!

5 AM next morning-

No, I certainly have *not* been out that late. It just happened that I got up early and remembered that I hadn't finished writing you. Well, its back to school I go today, and I do so wish Ruth was going to be there. We did have such fun together last year.

I guess I better stop now and try and go to sleep again. Hope the snap is all right. Do write soon, please, as I'm 'fraid its going to be very lonely in school.

Much love,
Deenie

from Mount Vernon Seminary

Oct 19, 1938

Peale dearest,

Will you please forgive me for not writing you sooner? You see, I have so much math to make up that I spend every spare moment in the book. It really was grand of you to write me even tho I didn't write you and it meant an awful lot to me to hear from "the outside world!" Thanx loads.

I can't let you know right now about the game 'cause I'm not sure if I get a week-end. You see, we only get one weekend a term, and I don't know if I get that this year, 'cause I was so late. It sounds just perfect, and I do hope I can come. Cross your fingers for me!

Your letters *do* help an awful lot and it's just grand hearing from you. I just hope mine do the same. The only thing we look forward to in the morning is the mail and we practically go stark, staring mad if we don't get some.

My birthday is on December 9th, worse luck. It really is much too near Christmas. By the by, you might tell me when yours is too!!

There is a girl down here who would like very much to

meet Charles Bauer. She is going to be my room-mate soon, I hope. Her name is Lois Middleton and she's 5'4" with blonde hair and blue eyes and a southern accent. She comes from Charleston, S. C. She really is awfully sweet and full of fun and I'm sure Charles will like her very much. She was going to put a PS on this letter but she's going to class so she'll do it on the next one. Is Charles a Theta Chi?

Has Doug come back yet? Its too bad he's sick. Next time you write him, (if you do) give him my best. I wonder if this correspondence we are starting will turn out like the last one did. Remember? By the way, when is Charles coming down? You see, we have to get him on our lists (calling). Let us know a little ahead of time as there might be a slight bit of persuading to do.

As I've got a math class in ¾ hrs. I've got to do my homework. Good idea, I think. I'll be back after lunch.

Now that you've started on Lois and Charles, there is another girl here who would like to hear from one of your frat brothers (if you can find one that likes to write letters). She is as tall as I am with dark hair with blue eyes. She is another Southern lassie, from Alabama. You met her at the prom here. Her name is Louise DeBardeleben. Remember? She says she remembers dancing with you and for me to say "hello" to you for her.

I did an awful thing this summer. I didn't write Lee all summer. Gee I felt awful when I came back. I wrote him yesterday and I do hope he isn't mad at me.

This letter seems to have lasted all day. It started in the morning and here it is 10:00 and I've been writing by candle light the last paragraph. Darn it, I'm sleepy, so you just have to excuse me if I sign off now, with

Much love,
Deenie
PS Write soon.

from Mount Vernon Seminary

Oct 21, 1938

Peale dearest,

As I owe you another letter, here it is. I'm 'fraid this one won't be very long tho, for the simple reason that there isn't much to say. The only important thing is this: I'm afraid I won't be able to come up on the eleventh 'cause we only get out Thanksgiving week-end. I'm terribly sorry, but I really can't make it, darn it all. I'll be out on Long Island from the Wednesday before Thanksgiving to the Sunday after. Do you think you could drop in and say hello sometime? Anyway call me up sometime out there. Telephone number is Roslyn 674. OK?

I hope you got my other letter. You said you were hoping to hear from me Monday, so I felt sorry for you and sent you a "special." Hope you didn't mind.

We are going to have a fashion show out here tomorrow night. I saved all of thirty-five {cents} by being tall. You see, all of the models are short, and one of the evening-dresses is too long, so they asked me to wear it. That's the only time in my life I've been glad to be tall.

My math book is calling me. We have a test tomorrow, so I better start studying. Write soon.

Much love,

Deenie

PS Please excuse short letter.

from Mount Vernon Seminary

Oct. 24, 1938

Dearest Peale,

Thanx so much for the long book. It really does need to be bound. I hope you'll excuse the writing, but you see, I'm in chapel. Remember last year? Many is the letter that has been written in chapel. The only difference is that I'm not in the choir this year. Oh, darn it. They just played and sang the same hymn that they sang the week-end you and Doug came down. I was in a very mournful frame of mind anyway, and that just finished me. Why, I do believe I'm going sentimental on myself. Forgive me please. They shouldn't have played that hymn.

To go back to what I started to say, your letter really was grand. I'm so *so* sorry I can't come up, but it is not humanly possible. You know I would if I could. I just thought of something! (No cracks) Mother is coming down that week-end. Maybe I could do a bit of light persuasion. Don't give up the ship yet. Something might happen. If I did come, Mrs. Tyler would have to come with me. I hope you won't mind, but I'm afraid it will have to be. You know!

Well, I've been up to mischief again. Yesterday at the horse-show between the American, Mexican and Chilean Army, Midge (one of our hosts) and I decided we would go and see her friend, who is captain of the Chilean team. So off we trotted (we would) and looked him up and decided we'd ask him and another one to go to a concert with us. So we did, and have been having an awful time trying to fix it up. Wouldn't you know I'd get in a jam only one week after I came? Just like me. I'm 'fraid I'll never be an angel.

The sermon is ending, so I gotta go. Bye-bye, and write soon.
Much love,
Deenie

to Charles

Glad to hear that we're going to correspond with each other. Make it snappy!

Lois

from Mount Vernon Seminary

Oct. 26, 1938
Peale dearest,

For once, I'm not writing this in chapel. I'm most annoyed but it seems to be true. And now, I'll try and answer all the questions you asked me.

I'll have to let you know about the Spring prom. Mother is coming down this week-end and I can ask her then. I'm afraid she'll say, "No, you're much too young to go to a college prom!" Well, at least I can try anyway. There's no harm in that. I hope she'll loosen up on me a little this year. Where is it? What is the date?

Yes, do send me a copy of "the Banter." I think it would be very amusing to see. If there is anything worthwhile in our "Cloister Columns," I'll send you a copy of that. I doubt if it will be very good, it hardly ever is, but I'll see anyway.

Tee Dee says "grand!" to J. Newhart. She may be coming home with me for Thanksgiving so you'll meet her if you come down. She has already taken her week-end up to West-Point, so her Mother is going to apply a slight bit of pressure and see if she can get out. I hope so, cause she really is an awfully nice kid.

What do I have to do or haven't to do to become a sister? Please enlighten me a bit on the subject so I won't do anything wrong.

Three guesses what happened to me! I was made a member of the French Club! I've never been so surprised in my life as when I got a polite little note in my mailbox asking me to join. My French can pass, but it is not *that* good!

Do you remember that little episode I wrote you about the Chilean Army officers? Well, we really got in trouble about that. The teachers took it the wrong way and we got blown sky-high. Oh well, it's all in a day's work!

Honestly, Peale, I'm going to tie my fingers crossed till this week-end. Mom's just *got* to let me come up for that prom. We'd have such fun together.

No, I haven't heard anything from Doug, but get news bulletins from Ruth every single letter she writes. It seems to me that the love-bug has bitten her good and hard.

I've got to run along now, to listen to a talk on birds. Sounds so interesting I'll probably take 40 winks while it's going on. Write soon and don't forget to answer my questions.

Much love,
Deenie

from Mount Vernon Seminary

Nov. 1, 1938
(On the back of the envelope)
Sit down before you read this or you might fall down. Don't read this if you're in a bad frame of mind.

Peale dearest,

Thanx so much for your two letters. Now, please prepare yourself for some very bad news. First of all, I can't come up on the 11th 'cause we only get one week-end and Mother has planned for me to take it on Thanksgiving. I'm awfully sorry, but there isn't really anything I can do about it. Next, I can't make the spring prom as I already have a date for another one. You see, someone else had your bright idea, too. Also, Mother wouldn't have said yes cause I'm not old enough to go to a college-prom, darn it all, 'cause you know how much I'd love to come. Now comes the last, but not least. Do you remember that ring I had last year? Well, I still feel the same way about it, and I guess that makes me ineligible to Theta-Chi. Don't you think so?

Honest, Peale, you don't know how I've hated writing all this to you, but I don't think it would have been fair to you not to have told you. I'm really terribly sorry, but it had to be done sooner or later. And now, to be a bit more cheerful, when do you have free time Thanksgiving? I may be able to see you then and I do hope so.

I heard (never mind from who) that Doug has been in school all year. Is that true? I also heard that he is stringing her along. I hope with all my heart that's not true, cause you know how much I like Ruth and I'd hate for anything like that to happen to her.

Please write soon and try not to be simply furious with me.
Much love,
Deenie

from Mount Vernon Seminary

Nov. 3, 1938
Wed. evening
Peale dearest,

It was really grand to hear your voice last nite. The reason I thought it was Dad was because he was the only person I think of that would call me and also, I couldn't hear very well as there were about twelve girls in the room next to me that were screaming and yelling. Anyway, thanx loads for calling.

I'm so sorry I couldn't make that week-end. We could have had such fun. You mentioned in one of your letters something about Skytop. Yes, we are going again this year and we're hoping for some nice cold weather. Think you could try again this year? It's pretty far off to plan about, but just keep it in the back of your mind and let me know about it later.

I'm going down to South Carolina for Christmas, but I'm coming up to NY around the first. Maybe I could see you before you go back to school and before I do too. But I better stop running on about all these plans in the future when I've really got to come back to the present and stop writing. I've got homework to do.

Nite!
Much love,
Deenie

from Mount Vernon Seminary

Nov. 13, 1938
Peale dearest,

Please excuse the paper but I've run out and I'm borrowing Lois'. Speaking of Lois, she wants to know when Charles is going to write her.

Also, please excuse the writing 'cause I'm extremely nervous at this point. In fifteen minutes I've got to go down and see the Pres. and he's going to tell me if I can go see Mummy off. He's just *got* to let me go. It'll be the last time I'll see her for six months, maybe more, and that's an awfully long time.

To get back to a slightly calmer frame of mind, if that's possible right now, of course you are forgiven. Yes, I still have the pledge-pin and I'll keep it if you want me to. I'm so glad you aren't mad at me. Well the fifteen minutes have passed and I've got to go. Keep your fingers crossed! Well, I'm back and we're in exactly the same place we started from. At least I'm not quite so jittery and that is a help.

I'll think about you this week-end and wish I was with you. I do so wish that weekend had worked out, but it *was*, as you said, a little impossible.

It really would be swell if you could come up to Skytop. This year, we really *will* make it! (I hope!)

I've got to go as someone is coming to visit me. A gent at that too! Don't get green-eyed. He's over thirty. Nite! And much love,
Deenie
PS Mi scrive—quick!

from Mount Vernon Seminary

Nov. 16, 1938

Peale dearest,

I'm so sorry you didn't get my letter I sent to Boonton. Guess I mailed it a little too late.

I received Oswald and have become very attached to him already. I promise I'll take good care of him and see he's not lonely. I'm sure he'll not want for noise 'cause Lois and I have the reputation of being the noisiest pair in the school. You can hear us for miles. We had better keep quiet this week 'cause if we aren't, we're going to have to go to study hall in the evenings, which would be horrible! I hate to go to study hall.

I've decided that I'm going to try and be good this year and make Optima which is the honor society. I would have made it last year, but Ruthie and I were always getting marked off for something or other. If I do get in it, I'll be able to go out 12 hours a week-end instead of six. Here's hoping anyhow.

Only seven more days now, and we'll be out. That really will be grand. And only two more weekends after that till Christmas vacation. Some fun. I'm afraid the time will drag, tho.

I've got to do two days lessons in 2 hours so I better start. Thanx again for Oswald. I'll take good care of him. Write soon.

Much love,
Deenie

from The Plaza

Jan. 5, 1939
The Plaza
Fifth Avenue at 59th Street
New York
Peale dearest,

Please forgive me for not writing sooner than this, but I've been going every minute for the last three days. Also please excuse the pencil and writing. You see, I'm on the train on the way to Washington to school and trains will be trains, you know.

Honestly Peale, I can't thank you enough for the white angora gloves and the little charms. As soon as we get to Washington I'm going to get them put on. You were a dear to send them to me and I really can't tell you how much I like them. As a matter of fact, I didn't find the charms till two days later. I put them on one evening and felt something hard in the fingers and couldn't figure out what it was. Did I get a big surprise!

Now about Skytop. We are going up *either* the fourth *or* the seventeenth. In other words, if there is no snow on the fourth then we'll try again on the seventeenth. Do you remember what happened last year? We're making sure it doesn't happen again. Darn good idea, I think.

I missed you at that dance on the second, but I could see your point in not coming. I really shouldn't have asked you in the first place but you know me. I never think of the in's and out's of a thing.

Here we are in Baltimore already. It really doesn't seem as if I've been gone for three hours. Only three more hours of freedom and then I'll be back in the dear old cemetery. Cheerful thought, isn't it?

It will be such fun to see you up at Skytop. I'm looking forward to your meeting Lois. You'll like her just as much as you did Ruth.

I gotta go but do write soon.

Much love,

Deenie

from Mount Vernon Seminary

Jan 12, 1939

Peale Dearest,

Please forgive me for not writing sooner and more often. I know it was horrid of me.

First of all, I'm 'fraid this letter is going to have to answer both of your sweet ones. You see, I'm trying to make Optima which is the scholastic club here and that takes up almost every minute of the day. The requirements are three out of four honor rolls for your work and three out of four for your citizenship. If I make the darn thing, I'll be lucky.

First of all, who is Harry S? What happened to you that you couldn't write? To go on answering your questions, yes, it was too bad you didn't come to the dance. We could have had fun. About the Skytop trip, we will go on the third if there is snow. Otherwise, I'm 'fraid it will have to be the seventeenth. We'll hope not anyway. It will be fun to meet Johnny. We really will have a grand time up there if everything works out properly. Lois is still undecided whether she is going up, but we have made up *her* mind and she is. We better break the news to her gently, tho.

As to the picture, I guess you know the answer by now. Not till I get one taken and I can't say when that will be.

It would be swell to have you and your friend down here that weekend. Please send me the exact date and I'll fix things so we can see you. I'll have to get you on Lois' calling list too. On second thought, please send me your friend's name and I can get him on her list and that would eliminate all difficulties that might arise. Good idea, don't you think? I better warn you here and now. We will be chaperoned by Mrs. T. herself so don't be disappointed. Neither Lois or I are in the choir this year, so we can sit with you during chapel. Also, we only get six hours out, you know, so you'll just have to wander around here with us the rest of the time. A big thrill, I'm sure.

If you'll send me the date of your first exam, I'll send you a telegram like I did last year. I really don't see how it would do much good, but if it does, so much the better!

I really have to go now and study French, so do write soon.
Much love,
Deenie
PS Give Harry (who ever he is) my best. Is he Theta Chi too ?

from Mount Vernon Seminary

Jan 30, 1939
Peale dearest,

Thanks so much for your grand letter. I'm so glad the telegram got to you in time. I sent it so late that I was afraid all your exams would be finished before it reached you.

Yes, we are really and truly going up to Skytop if the weather keeps cold. Anyway, I'll send you a telegram before we go so you'll be positive that we'll be there. I think our train gets in at eight. Will you let me know when you'll get there and then we can arrange a place where we can meet you. As to ice-skating, we're both game. Lois has been on them exactly once and I've only been on them three or four times, but we'll try anything once. Honestly, I just can't wait!! It'll be the first time that I've ever been in a place that has a lot of snow and ice. Also, I've only been on skis once and I'm kinda scared of them, but maybe I'll be able (with enough persuasion) to screw up my courage and try.

I talked to Mummy over the phone yesterday and she said she was going to bring the *Sea Cloud* over to Belgium in May and she was going up to Russia again. The general opinion is that there will be a war in Europe some time this spring. If it breaks while the *Sea Cloud* is over there, she'll be commandeered and that will be the last we'll see of her. I do so wish Mummy would leave well enough alone and leave her sitting safely in Jacksonville. I just couldn't bear to have anything happen to her.

I really should run along and study for that darn three-hour exam on Wednesday. Wish me luck!!

Love,

Deenie

from Mount Vernon Seminary

Feb 7, 1939
Monday
Peale dearest,

I tried to write you a letter Saturday night as you asked me to, but the results were pretty awful so I tore them up quick-like. I guess I was too darn sleepy to make any sense. We didn't get to sleep till about 2 'cause some of the kids insisted on staying in our room and talking. Finally we just kicked them out. I'm 'fraid it was awfully rude of us, but it went a slight bit too far. We dropped right off the minute our heads touched the pillows. We got up around eight-thirty in the morning and went out to have our pictures taken. I took another lovely tumble on my bad knee and am now sitting in bed with an ice bag!! To get back to what I was saying—we then went and tobogganed some more. We stayed out so long that we only had fifteen min. to change and pack. You should have seen the state the bags were in! We couldn't find anything this morning 'cause everything was so mussed up. I had to stand on the bags while Lois closed them.

The train ride back was horrible. Everyone was *so* sleepy and the train was *so* rough. When we got back to school we just tumbled in bed and fell asleep. No one had done any work and classes were something horrible. On the whole, it has been an awful day. Oh well, it was worth it! We *did* have such fun!

I've got to go and do some work now, 'cause I'm slightly behind! Much love,
Deenie

PS Lois and I send best to Johnnie. Lois sends her best to you and says she's sorry she couldn't see you to say good bye.

from Mount Vernon Seminary

Feb 16, 1939
Dearest Peale,

Thanks so much for the letters and the telegram! It was so cute. I'm so sorry I haven't written before this, but we've been so busy with rehearsals for a French play which we gave yesterday, thank goodness. I'm so glad the darn thing is over 'cause it had us all worked up to a white heat with all the rehearsals and what-not. I haven't had a free minute for the last two days. Oh well, its all over now, thank goodness.

I like your new mascot very much. He sounds full of the dickens. More power to him! By-the-by, just how many mascots do you have?

Poor Lois was in bed for a week with her head and she still can't use her eyes for more than an hour each day. She just had a very bad head-ache and it affected her eyes somehow. Poor kid. We all felt so sorry for her. She's OK now, thank goodness. Yes, everyone was so stiff when they got back that it really was torture to do Modern Dancing and play Basketball. It was worth it tho. I've still got a nice little souvenir which I'll have for a few more weeks I think. My bump! It's still purple tho it doesn't hurt very much any more. Lois and I are a fine pair. We both can't stand on our own two feet!

Mrs. Tyler is doing us a great big favor! She's going to get me out of school on Wednesday afternoon for a doctor's cut and a prom cut and a week-end. More fun. I'll be up in NY on Wed and Thurs night and on Friday morning, I'll be going up to Choate for the rest of the weekend.

Gotta go now, but do write soon.
Much love,
Deenie

from Mount Vernon Seminary

Mar. 2, 1939
Peale dear

I do hope you'll forgive me for not writing sooner than this, but you made a mistake about my week-end. It was this last one and I'm still busy making up work for the three days I missed. It was so sweet of you to write me that wonderful long letter. I honestly don't see how you could write it. I'm afraid I'm not going to be able to do anything spectacular like that, 'cause I just can't do it. Also, darn it all, these little blinkers of mine aren't acting the way they should and I went down to the oculist this afternoon and he put those crazy drops in them that make the pupils dilate and I can't see a foot in front of me, thus the horrible writing. Please excuse it 'cause there's nothing I can do about it.

It sounded as if you really had . . . (letter torn and missing a part) . . . see my mother off to Europe a few months ago. Isn't that sweet of them. Yes, I really had a grand time up at Choate, with Jim. I do want you to meet him sometime 'cause he is . . .

(letter torn and missing the rest)

from Mount Vernon Seminary

May 13, 1939
Peale dear,

Thanx so much for the letter. I'm 'fraid this going to be a very short note 'cause it's about the end of the only free period I have today. Now that commencement time is drawing near, there is so darn much work to do that I can't seem to find time to get any letters written. I think I must owe about twenty-five or thirty letters and some of them from three weeks back. Isn't that dreadful?

I hope you pass that exam. It doesn't sound so easy. I've got four to take but they only cover one year's work and that's bad enough. Only a little over two weeks now and school will be over for the year!! I just can't believe it's such a short time.

I hope that Lois is going to come home with me for a while. It would be wonderful if she could.

I got a letter from Lee and he said he hadn't heard from you in ages. What's wrong?

The bell's rung so I've got to run along. Please write.

Love,

Deenie

Dina Merrill, born Nedenia Marjorie Hutton, was daughter of the heiress Marjorie Merriweather Post and the financier Edward Francis Hutton known as E. F. Hutton. Born in New York City, she attended Mount Vernon Seminary in Washington, DC and the American Academy of Dramatic Arts in NYC. Actress, heiress, socialite, businesswoman, and philanthropist, she divorced Stanley Rumbough Jr. and Cliff Robertson, marrying Ted Hartley in 1989. She pursued an accomplished movie, television, and stage career from 1957 to 2003

Definitions

bellhop/steward—member of the crew involved in providing personal services to passengers; steward more related to commissary or food services

black gang—crew members who work in the engine room, boiler room, or fire room; so called because they would be covered in coal dust during the days of coal-fired steamships

bo'sun—a boatswain or non-commissioned officer responsible for the deck department on a ship (hull maintenance, rigging, anchors, boats)

bridge—command center of a ship

buntline, clewline—one of the ropes attached to the foot of a square sail to haul it up to the yard for furling

outhaul—running rigging attached to sails to raise, lower, tighten and loosen them from the deck

chief engineer—in charge of the engineering department of a ship; responsible for all operation and maintenance of any and all engineering equipment (motors, generators, propulsion plant)

clews—outer corners of a sail

coolie—unskilled laborer; in South Asia, especially a porter

deck gang—crew members involved in mooring, anchoring, sailing, and general deck maintenance

donkey engine—small auxiliary engine

fo'c'sle—forecastle or forward part of a ship below the deck; holds anchor machinery and sailor's living quarters

forepeak—part of the hold of a ship within the angle of the bow

hard over—command given to bring the rudder all the way starboard or port

hold or cargo hold—area below deck where cargo is placed for transportation by the ship

knot—a unit of speed at sea equaling one nautical mile per hour, equivalent to 1.15 MPH

lee or leeward—downwind side of the ship

lighter—barge used to transfer goods and passengers to and from anchored ships

make fast—tie up, as lines from a ship to the pier

mizzen mast—one of four masts on a four-masted square rigger, including, from fore to aft, the fore, main, mizzen, and spanker masts

paid off—action of having been paid wages due on discharge

quartermaster—individual on watch on the bridge of a ship responsible for navigation and keeping the log

radioman—crew member responsible for ship-to-shore electronic communications

ratlines—rope rungs fastened between lines of permanent rigging that go from the deck to the mast to form ladders enabling access to the topmasts and yards

reefing—reducing the area of a sail

reeve—to pass a line through a block or pulley

rickshaw—two-wheeled passenger cart, generally pulled by one man and carrying one passenger

scupper—an opening in the side of a ship at deck level to allow water to run off. Over time, water causes the metal to rust, hence the "rusty scupper."

shrouds—rigging supporting a mast running fore and aft

sideboy—seaman who helps dignitaries/guests board or depart a ship

sluice box—long, narrow channel that water passes through when separating and recovering gold from gravel by the use of running water

square rigger—a sailing ship where the primary sails are carried on horizontal spars or yards which are perpendicular, or square, to the masts

spar—pole used to support rigging and sails. All masts are spars, but not all spars are masts. Spars include booms, yards, bowsprits

stays—rigging supporting a mast from side to side

to'gallant—one of the square sails on a square rigger, including, from bottom to top, the main (or course), topsail, top gallant, royal, and sky sails. Topsails and topgallants may be split into upper and lower topsail and upper and lower topgallant.

warp—to maneuver a ship into or out of a dock or pier using mooring lines and the engine

whip—to tie off the end of a line to keep it from unraveling

windward—upwind side of the ship

well deck—deck below the main deck

yard—horizontal spar from which a square sail is suspended

yardarm—very end of a yard

ship command

captain—person in command of a vessel

first mate—second in command of a commercial vessel

second mate—third in command (head of deck department)

third mate—fourth in command (licensed member of deck department)

ship geography

bow—the ship's front

stern—the ship's rear

starboard—the ship's right

port—the ship's left

Acknowledgments
from Harry Peale Haldt III

Thank you to my grandparents and parents for saving so many letters and photographs I uncovered while going through boxes of family records and files to add visuals to my father's once-lost manuscript.

Thank you to my wife, Susan, for time she spent looking through family records with me, making suggestions on which pictures, letters, and brochures made sense to include, and countless hours proofreading sections from the publisher. I am grateful for her invaluable encouragement and support right from the beginning when we found the file with Dad's draft and as we went forward realizing his dream to publish his stories.

Thanks to Marcia Gagliardi, publisher at Haley's and my friend from Quabbin Valley Pro Musica, our local classical music singing group, for her enthusiasm about the book.

Finally, thanks to my dad for taking the time to write the stories he remembered. I'm glad he listened to people who told him, "You ought to write a book."

About the Author and Editor

H. Peale Haldt Jr., called Peale

The late Harry Peale Haldt Jr, known as Peale, was born in Ridley Park, Pennsylvania in 1916. He grew up in Boonton, New Jersey, and distinguished himself as a track star at Boonton High School. He graduated from Colgate University in 1939. He served as a technical sergeant in the army in Europe during World War II. Peale began his sales career with Huron Milling Company in New York and retired to Florida after twenty years as marketing manager, Food Ingredients Division, Nestle USA, White Plains, New York. He and his wife, Barbara Anita Myers, had two children, Joanne, or Jody, of Gloucester, Massachusetts, and Harry.

Harry Peale Haldt III, known as Harry or Trip, entered the navy through Officer Candidate School, Newport, Rhode Island, after graduation from Colgate University in 1968. He served aboard the USS *Tripoli* (LPH-10) in the Pacific as assistant combat information center officer during the Vietnam War. He retired as Captain, United States Naval Reserve, in 1995.

Captain Harry P. Haldt III US Navy (retired)

After leaving active service, he entered the business world as a credit trainee at Chase Manhattan Bank in New York and retired from banking after thirty-nine years as assistant vice-president/branch manager at Citizens Bank in West Pawlet, Vermont.

Married to Susan Christina Flannagan, he lives in Athol, Massachusetts, where he is active in the Athol Lions Club and sings with and serves as manager for Quabbin Valley Pro Musica, resident chorus of the 1794 Meetinghouse, Inc. He has a daughter, Christina Haldt, three stepsons, Tom, Liam, and Paddy Flannagan, and five grandchildren.

He compiled the stories and illustrations for and edited *Upper To' Gallants and Rusty Scuppers* to entertain readers and as a tribute to his dad.

Colophon

Text for *Upper To'gallants and Rusty Scuppers* was set in Mrs. Eaves OT, designed in 2002 by Zuzana Licko of Emigre type foundry. The font takes its name from Sarah Eaves, the woman who became the wife of John Baskerville, 1707–1775, a printer and type designer.

As Baskerville set up his printing and type business, Mrs. Eaves moved in with him as a live-in housekeeper, eventually becoming his wife after the death of her first husband. Like the widows of the type designers Caslon and Bodoni and the daughters of the typesetter Fournier, Sarah completed printing unfinished volumes that Baskerville left upon his death.

Titles and captions for *Upper To'gallants and Rusty Scuppers* are set in Avenir Next, designed in 1988 for Linotype by Adrian Frutiger. The original release of Avenir has weights grouped very close together with the difference barely distinguishable. In his autobiography, Frutiger explains his reasoning for the grouping decision as a response to the effects of how people perceive colour.

Between 2004 and 2007, Frutiger and Linotype's in-house type designer Akira Kobayashi reworked the Avenir family as Avenir Next to expand the range of weights and features.

www.ingramcontent.com/pod-product-compliance
Lightning Source LLC
Chambersburg PA
CBHW042132160426
43199CB00021B/2880